Fiction

From Sadie's Sketchbook
Shades of Truth (Book One)
Flickering Hope (Book Two)
Waves of Light (Book Three)
Brilliant Hues (Book Four)

The Girls of Harbor View
Girl Power (Book One)
Take Charge (Book Two)
Raising Faith (Book Three)
Secret Admirer (Book Four)

Boarding School Mysteries
Vanished (Book One)
Betrayed (Book Two)
Burned (Book Three)
Poisoned (Book Four)

Nonfiction

Faithgirlz Handbook
Faithgirlz Journal
Food, Faith, and Fun! Faithgirlz Cookbook
No Boys Allowed
What's a Girl to Do?
Girlz Rock
Chick Chat
Real Girls of the Bible
My Beautiful Daughter

Check out www.faithgirlz.com

faithGirlz!
the beauty of believing

You!
A Christian Girl's Guide to Growing Up
REVISED EDITION

Nancy
Rue

ZONDERVAN®

ZONDERVAN.com/
AUTHORTRACKER
follow your favorite authors

ZONDERKIDZ
www.zonderkidz.com

You! A Christian Girl's Guide to Growing Up

This title is also available as a Zondervan ebook.
Visit www.zondervan.com/ebooks

Requests for information should be addressed to:

Zonderkidz, 5300 Patterson Ave. SE, Grand Rapids, Michigan 49530

Library of Congress Cataloging-in-Publication Data

Rue, Nancy N.
     You! : a Christian girl's guide to growing up / Nancy Rue.
          pages cm. — (Faithgirlz!)
     ISBN 978-0-310-73319-5 (softcover)
     1. Girls—Religious life—Juvenile literature. 2. Girls—Conduct of life—Juvenile
literature. 3. Adolescence—Religious aspects—Christianity—Juvenile literature. I.
Title.
BV4551.3.R845 2013
248.8'2—dc23   2012041255

Published in association with the literary agency of Alive Communications, Inc., 7680
Goddard Street, Suite 200, Colorado Springs, CO 80920. www.alivecommunications.com

Zonderkidz is a trademark of Zondervan.

Interior Design: Sarah Molegraaf

Printed in the United States

22 /DCI/ 20 19 18 17 16 15

This book is dedicated to the thirty-four mini-women from the *Tween You and Me* blog who shared themselves honestly so that other girls like them could live their way joyfully and beautifully into young womanhood. I couldn't have written this book without them.

Contents

PART II: BEAUTY MATTERS

How to Read This Book

This book is bursting with stuff you need to know about growing up. It's set up so you'll be able to find exactly what you need. Here's how::

HERE'S THE DEAL ...

Tons of information about all the areas of puberty and beauty care. This comes from questions mini-women have asked me and that I know you're probably wondering about too.

That Is SO Me!

Quizzes to help you figure out where you are on things like choosing a bra and dealing with body odor, picking out your clothes and figuring out the whole inner-beauty thing. These are the kind of tests you don't have to study for—and there are no grades!

GOT GOD?

What God tells us about taking care of our bodies, about physical appearance, and about being lovely inside.

You'll be amazed what the Bible (yeah, the BIBLE!) says about the things you're dealing with. You'll also find out how to talk to God about it, especially when you're feeling way too awkward to discuss it with anyone else.

YOU CAN DO IT

An artsy-craftsy way for you to try out what you've just read. And not just you, but you AND your friends. This is fun stuff you can bring your BFFs in on too—if you want. (That only makes sense, right?)

That's What I'm Talkin' About

A place for you to fill in some blanks about your own body and beauty thoughts—or draw or doodle—or even journal if you really have a lot to say.

MINI-WOMEN SAY

> " Quotes from tween girls like you who say some things so much better than I can. "

Just So You Know

Fun facts to make you feel smarter. (They're good things to talk about when you want to steer the conversation away from who's fat and who has ape legs and who wears lame clothes!)

Who, ME?

Things you can do super fast to help you see how all this body and beauty information fits YOU.

All right, then, let's get started!

Part I: Body Talk

1

I'm a What? A Mini-Woman?

If you're a girl between eight and twelve years old, you're actually a **mini-woman**. You get that, right? You're no longer totally a "little girl" (as in, you can make your own peanut butter sandwich), and you haven't completely lost your mind yet and become a teenager (although I suspect there's some eye-rolling and "whatevering" already going on).

Some people call that being a "tween." I like the term *mini-woman*, though, and here's why:

You've probably noticed some changes going on with your body these days. Like ... it's not the same as it was a year ago. Or a month ago. Or even *yesterday*.

That's not your imagination going wild. The only other

time in your life when this much different stuff happened in such a short period was between the day you were born and your first birthday. Since then you've been able to depend on your body to be the same old reliable bod every day except for growing taller. And then it seemed like overnight you were turning into somebody else!

One of your fellow mini-women talks about it this way:

> You know what scares me? HORMONES. I'm not exactly sure what they are, but when people talk about them, they sound bad. I think that's what causes periods (but I'm not sure). I also hear that's what makes you, like, emotional too, and if so, I HATE hormones!

She's right about one thing: **Hormones** do cause periods and changes in emotions and just about everything else that's taking you by surprise right now (or will soon).

> The emotions are weird. I never thought when I was little I'd act the way I did today. And also the HAIR. I never thought I'd have all this hair in scary places.

When your body starts to make those new and different hormones, you go through a stage in your life called **puberty**. It's actually a good thing because it means you're slowly turning into a woman. And since you're a smaller version of a grown-up woman, well, that makes you a mini-woman.

"A *woman*?" you say. "I'm having enough trouble being a *kid*!"

Yeah, I know. On top of more homework and harder math and more complicated drama going on with friends, you have to deal with bras, hairy armpits, and feet that are suddenly too big for the rest of you. What was God thinking when he put *that* all together, right?

Actually, God did all of us women a favor by making puberty a gradual process. Wouldn't it be freaky to go to bed one night looking like you're seven and wake up the next morning with the body of an eighteen-year-old? It's way better that it works like it does.

66 All I have to say is, boys are sooo lucky. 99

That's a lot of change, but it isn't everything that's going on with you in these becoming-a-mini-woman years.

Most girls your age also start thinking about the way they *look*. For some, that's a complete blast. Clothes! Fun hairstyles! Nail polish … pierced ears … the list goes on. For others, it's a downer. They feel funky and not very trendy and just plain unlovely even though none of the above is actually true. Whichever sounds more like you (and that probably changes from day to day … hour to hour …), caring about whether you're pretty, cute, or even just not a gorilla is absolutely normal. Yeah, normal, but often confusing and hard and even painful.

Put it all together—body changes and beauty issues—and, yikes, it could also be just plain scary. But it doesn't have to be, and that's why you have this book in your hands. It's divided into two sections, "Body Talk" and "Beauty Matters." Each will help you through all the changes that are going on in you right now, and will do it in a way that's unique to your own God-made, mini-woman self. There's so much that's great about being a girl. Why let the hard parts send you into a funk?

In the "Body Talk" section, you'll find out that even the toughest things about puberty can be a whole lot easier if you:

○ have all the facts and understand what's going on and why.

○ are prepared with the right supplies.

○ find out who's the most helpful in getting you through all this (definitely including God).

○ actually *like* the body that's changing you daily into the woman you were made to be.

In the "Beauty Matters" section, you'll find help to:

○ decide how important looking good is to YOU.

○ discover your unique beauty (which everybody has).

○ learn ways to get that only-you beauty shining.

○ accept the things about your appearance that you can't change (and maybe even learn to love them!).

○ understand what inner beauty is and let it be the most beautiful thing about you.

I've had a lot of help from mini-women who, like you, are in the middle of this turning-into-a-woman process even as we speak. You'll read their true stories here in "Mini-Women Say" and you'll know you are SO not alone. I like to think we're on a journey together. Some of the steps we'll take will apply to everybody. Some will be unique to just you. And always, always, we'll have God out ahead of us, showing us the way many mini-women have traveled before us—and making it better than ever.

You ready? Then let's talk body.

2

What's Happening to My BODY?!

On the *Tween You and Me* blog recently, we were talking about the things that are scary about puberty. One mini-woman wrote:

> I don't think I'm scared about anything in particular, but sometimes I worry about what I don't know.

That's so right, isn't it? We get way more worked up when we don't actually know what this new thing is that we're facing. So let's start with some facts that will help you be worry free.

HERE'S THE DEAL ON WHAT PUBERTY IS

Puberty transforms you from a flat-chested, smooth-as-a-pear little girl to a miniature woman with ...

- breasts.

- new hair under the arms and in the pubic area (y'know, between your legs).

- thicker, coarser hair, on the legs especially (so lovely, right?).

- sweat that has a less-than-lovely odor (a fact your brother is more than happy to point out to you).

- wider hips (as in, your jeans no longer fit).

- a taller, maybe even heftier, body (just when you start caring about being skinny).

Who, ME?

Put a question mark next to any or all of the things on that list above that YOU have, well, questions about.

"What I don't get is that in theory, once you have your period, you can have a baby. But looking down at my body, there is no way I could have one. I'm also wondering if my chest is going to grow any more or what?"

You may ask, "And this happens because ... ?" There really is a reason! It's a little complicated, so here it is in simple form.

- Every female's body is designed to automatically start producing two new hormones at some time in the tween years (though later for some girls). Those are **estrogen** and **progesterone**. Estrogen causes all of the stuff on page 24. Progesterone, with some help from estrogen, causes and controls **menstrual periods**, which happen once a month. More on those later.

- As if that weren't enough, the arrival of these new hormones also leads to some emotional changes.

- Mood swings: You've got the giggles one minute, and the next you're crying, all for no apparent reason. You can feel like your feelings are out of control (even though they're not).

- Changes in your attitude about boys: Where once you were convinced they were all possessed by demons, or at the very least had cooties, you find yourself wanting to look cute for them. Or you secretly enjoy it when the one least likely to actually *have* cooties unties your sneaker for the forty-third time.

- A new need to have more privacy, especially when you're getting dressed or taking a shower. (And even more especially if you have brothers in the house ...)

> **66** What I didn't expect is that I'm way more 'private' about my body parts than I used to be. It used to be okay if somebody in my family walked in on me when I was in the shower, but now it just isn't! **99**

Now that you know you're normal and that this stuff happens to every girl on the planet, let's look at how you're unique in the way it's going to all play out.

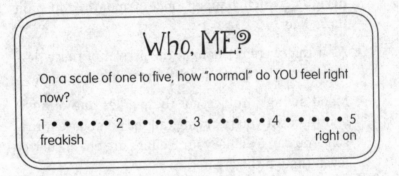

Who, ME?

On a scale of one to five, how "normal" do YOU feel right now?

1 • • • • • 2 • • • • • 3 • • • • • 4 • • • • • 5
freakish   right on

That Is SO Me!

Not everybody experiences puberty at the same time in their lives or in exactly the same way because God made everyone unique, right down to her hormones. The following quiz will show you where you are on the changing-into-a-woman journey. As you take the quiz, remember that you aren't "behind" or "ahead" of anybody else. You're right where YOU are supposed to be.

Which of these descriptions sounds MOST like your body right now? Not everything will match you exactly, of course, so pick the one that's closest.

○ **Girl One**: No hair has shown up yet in her armpits or between her legs (pubic area). There don't appear to be any breasts in her immediate future, and her waistline is the same as it always was. Her hips haven't changed either. As for the hair on her legs, she doesn't really see much. There's never anything on her underwear when she takes her panties off.

○ **Girl Two**: She's noticed some hair sprouting in her armpits and pubic area, and the hair on her legs has gotten thicker and coarser than it used to be. She may or may not be wearing a bra yet, but she does have little raised bumps or pointy little mounds that will someday be breasts. Her waist feels kind of thick, and her hips have spread so that sometimes she feels, well, fat. What's really different is that when she takes off her underwear, there's sometimes thick, clear stuff on them, or maybe a brownish stain.

○ **Girl Three**: She's had hair in her armpits and pubic area for a couple of months or more, and she's thinking she might want to shave her legs (if she isn't doing it already). She definitely has breasts that are round and pretty full, and maybe the area around her nipples has gotten darker. She actually has a real waist now, and it feels like her hips are finally in proportion to the rest of her body. Sometimes she discovers blood spots on her underwear; she might even be having periods.

Now let's look at what that means, which will help you use this book in a way that's just right for you.

If you're the most like Girl One, you haven't started puberty yet. Don't freak out! No matter how old you are, that's perfectly normal. Some girls start as early as eight or nine, while others don't start to see the signs until twelve or thirteen and in some cases even later. Reading this book will help you be ready when it does happen—and then you can enjoy the fun parts more.

If Girl Two resembles you, you're already in puberty even though you haven't started your period yet. This stage is where most of the surprises happen, so reading this book can be way helpful in walking you through those. It can even be fun. No, really.

Did Girl Three sound more like you? Then you're well on your way to young womanhood. In fact, you're probably getting used to the whole idea. But keep reading because this book will help you not only manage the changes, it will show you what's lovely about being a young woman.

One more time, remember this: Whether you are Girl One, Two, or Three, you are right where you're supposed to be at this very moment. If other girls tease you because you need a bra about as much as you need dentures or because you have more curves than a mountain road, they're showing their insecurities about their **own** bodies. As everyone starts to feel more comfortable with breasts and bras and periods, the teasing will slack off. (If it doesn't, you might want to read **Girl Politics** for some help with that.)

> Yesterday some boys said I am fat. NO, wait they YELLED it. My friends and family say I am not fat, but I'm starting to believe the boys.

Who, ME?

Has anybody teased YOU recently about your changing body? And, um, have YOU maybe made a joke about somebody else's pubescent self?

_____

_____

_____

_____

> It's kind of annoying that none of my really close friends my age have gotten their periods yet, and I got mine at eleven. They can't relate to what I'm going through with cramps and stuff.

HERE'S THE DEAL ABOUT THOSE DIFFERENCES

- Girls of different ethnic backgrounds start puberty at different times. For instance, the average African-American girl begins puberty just before the age of nine. The average white girl starts right before the age of ten. And remember, not everyone is "average."

- Pubic hair comes in all different thicknesses and colors and grows at different rates. It starts as straight, light-colored, fine hairs and grows in stages to the final darker and coarser curly hairs. Some of that depends on ethnic background too. Asian girls, for instance, seem to have less pubic hair.

- The "puberty growth spurt" starts at different ages for different girls. For some it seems to happen in a big way (from straight as a stick to lusciously curvy practically overnight), while for others it isn't as dramatic. In this two- to four-year time period, girls put on weight and grow taller at a faster rate than before (as much as four inches in a year instead of the average of two inches a year). The growth rate slows down by the time girls have their first period, and most girls reach their adult height one to three years after that. You may grow up to nine inches during the puberty growth spurt, but, again, some grow more and some grow less. It's all good!

- Your face will probably change some during puberty too. The lower part gets longer, and your chin juts out more. Your forehead gets wider. You'll actually start looking more like an adult than a kid, which is, of course, cool. Some girls' faces get sharper and more chiseled, and others' get fuller and look, well, older. If it seems like your face is staying its little-girl self, that's okay too. There is nothing wrong with having a young look.

- One of the most bizarre things about puberty is that the bones in your feet start to grow before other bones. That means your feet will reach their adult size before the rest of you does. Since everybody won't end up being the same height, everybody's feet aren't going to be the same size now either. Forget about comparing shoe sizes or worrying that you're going to feel like Ronald McDonald for the rest of your life. It will all balance out before you stop growing, and you *will* stop tripping every time you try to cross a room.

- During the growth spurt, your pelvic bones grow and fat grows around them, giving you hips. They make your waist seem smaller, and when your breasts develop—ta da!—you have curves. You're born with a body type already programmed in to develop during puberty, and there are basically three:

  ○ **Endomorph**: round body with soft curves and a little more body fat (which is NOT a bad thing, no matter what those TV and magazine ads show you).

  ○ **Ectomorph**: slim body with fewer curves and more angles (not a bad thing either!).

  ○ **Mesomorph**: muscular body with wide shoulders and slim hips (just as girl-like as the other body types).

- The weight spurt and the growth spurt don't always happen at the same time. It's more like a seesaw. For a while you're adding pounds faster than you're adding inches; then for a while you're gaining inches faster than you're gaining pounds. Everybody's see-saw is moving at a different, personal rate, so there's no need to get hung up on feeling fat or thinking you're scrawny next to your friends.

• It may seem like your moods are always out of sync with your friends' moods. You sometimes feel like letting it all hang out in silliness, while one of your friends is stuck in a funk—or the other way around. Many of the roller coaster rides your moods and feelings take during puberty are caused by the new hormones your body's producing. Some girls (and some grown-up women) are really jolted around emotionally by their hormones, while others seem to ride right over them. It takes time for your body to adjust, so don't think you're a total drama queen next to your best friend who never sheds a tear. How your moods bounce around depends partly on the way you've always reacted to the things that happen around you. If you were born a sensitive baby, you're probably going to be extra sensitive during puberty. If you've been a toughie from birth, you'll more than likely be a little short-tempered in your puberty years and perhaps more rebellious than your weepier friends. If you've been laid back since day one, that will probably continue. Basically, who you are emotionally will seem to be magnified about a jillion times.

> **"** I'm more developed than most of the other girls my age, but I don't worry about it because I know pretty soon they'll catch up. Then I can help them. **"**

Who, ME?

How much have YOU grown in the last six months? If you don't have a mark on the wall, try thinking about the legs of your jeans!

_____

> " Whenever I weigh myself, I feel like I'm always gaining weight because I'm growing, and I'm gaining it from growing upwards, not sidewards, but it still makes me feel fat just seeing those numbers go up, even though people say I'm not fat and that I have curves. So I guess I'm still sorta, kinda skinny-ish-normal-ish. "

Who, ME?

Look at a picture of yourself when you were seven and then look in the mirror. How has YOUR face changed?

_____

_____

_____

Who, ME?

What's the most graceful (NOT!) thing YOU have done lately? Can you laugh about it? (I mean, come on, ya gotta admit it was funny!)

_____

_____

_____

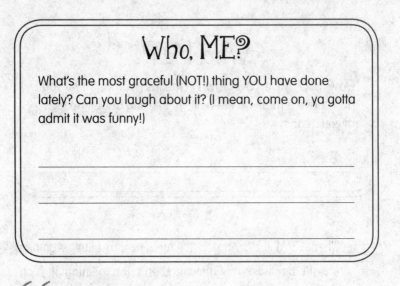 Now that I have curves, I can wear fashionable clothing better. Even though most of my friends are, like, cute little skinny things, I like being curvy.

I think if you put a boy's head on my body, you couldn't tell a difference. I am not developed at all!

Who, ME?

Put a star next to the body type above that best describes YOU.

Just So You Know

If you want a peek at how tall you might be when you're fully grown, try this:

1. Convert your birth father's height to inches.
   (6 feet tall = 72 inches)

2. Subtract 5 inches.

3. Convert your birth mother's height to inches.

4. Add it to #2.

5. Divide that by 2.

That should be close to your adult height.

> One day my mom took my best friend and me to Chik-Fil-A after school for dinner and I asked if I could have a milkshake, and she said no and I burst into tears like a two-year-old. I felt like an idiot in front of my friend who, like, doesn't have hormones yet, I guess.

Who, ME?

What did YOUR last meltdown look like?

_____

_____

Don't be surprised if at times you're not even sure how you're feeling!

But you'll get to know yourself better and be able to figure out just what's going on with you. For more about that, read *Everybody Tells Me to Be Myself, but I Don't Know Who I Am.*

If you weren't wondering before what you're going to do with all these changes, you probably are now! Before we go there, let's go to God, who set this whole thing in motion to begin with.

GOT GOD?

It's a good thing you don't have to go it alone. Even if you aren't particularly *thankful* for that right now, just know that there are three truths you can depend on from God.

Truth #1: God wants you to become a woman. And not just any woman, but one different from all others.

> Sixty queens there may be,
>
> and eighty concubines,
>
> and virgins beyond number;
>
> but my dove, my perfect one, is unique.

Song of Songs 6:8–9

Truth #2: God knows how strange and frustrating and often embarrassing and sometimes even painful the process of becoming that woman can be. God understands that it's a big deal. He's been hearing about it forever.

> We have a little sister,
>
> and her breasts are not yet grown.
>
> What shall we do for our sister?
>
> Song of Songs 8:8

(And you thought *your* siblings were up in your business!)

Truth #3: God listens to you when you have complaints and doubts and fears about this whole puberty thing. Jesus says there's nothing too small to pray about.

> "Are not two sparrows sold for a penny? Yet not one of them will fall to the ground outside your Father's care. And even the very hairs of your head are all numbered. So don't be afraid; you are worth more than many sparrows."
>
> Matthew 10:29–31

Puberty's a lot to handle, and we don't have any choice about going through it. But God never gives us anything to deal with that he doesn't also give us the tools for.

● ●

❝ I don't talk to anyone about body changes, really, except God. I know that may sound weird, but it's true! And helpful!! ❞

One of those tools is absolutely having someone you can talk to in addition to God. Sure, it can be embarrassing to even discuss your fears and confusion with your mom. But the more you do it, the easier it will be and the more *actual* information you'll get (instead of "I heard this was true" at Friday-night sleepovers). You'll find suggestions in this book for how to approach your mom or another adult woman you trust.

Who, ME?

Who do YOU talk to when the puberty path gets all twisty and weird?

_____

_____

66 I don't really talk about any of this, but if absolutely necessary, I would talk to my mom. Maybe. 99

The other people you can go to for support (though probably not for facts) are your friends, so let's start there.

66 Friends are easier to talk to, but Mom knows so much more than we do. I go to both for different reasons. 99

YOU CAN DO IT

Creating a Sisterhood, Part 1

Since EVERY girl has to walk the puberty path, you're all walking it together, right? So it makes sense to form a "sisterhood" so that you and your friends can not only reassure yourselves that all of you are normal-for-you, but you'll also be able to bolster each other up when things gets challenging and celebrate the way-cool parts of being mini-women. Besides, you're always going to need a support group of women in your life, so now is a great time to learn how to do that.

1. *Call a gathering of "sisters."* This can be you and your best friend, a circle of four or five girls you usually hang out with, or a new pair or bunch that comes together because you all need to. (God often arranges that.)

2. *Gather in a place where there won't be any male interference.* Enlist your mom's help in steering brothers, and even fathers, away. Everybody needs to feel comfortable talking about whatever comes up.

3. *Have this book on hand*, in case you have questions nobody knows the answer to.

4. *Explain that since everybody's body is changing right now, you want to create a sisterhood,* a safe group where you can share your experiences and anxieties and joys of going through puberty. Assure anybody who doesn't feel okay that she's not going to be shunned if she doesn't want to talk. It's fine if she just listens.

5. *Lay some ground rules:* Whatever is said in the group isn't to be spread around—especially to boys! No teasing. No comparing to each other.

6. *Try this activity for your first meeting:* Turn to pages 27 and 28 and ask the other girl(s) to listen and decide which **Girl** is most like them. If they want to share their answers they can, or you can simply read the explanations (or take turns doing that). If everybody's feeling at ease, you can share embarrassing moments that have happened with bras, periods, uncoordination, or emotional roller coasters. OR you can have people write those down and pull them out of a bowl and take turns reading them.

7. *Decide how you want to support each other from now on.* You don't have to meet on a regular basis. In fact, if you already hang out together, it will just come naturally from now on. You can also agree to get together when somebody has a special problem or hits a new milestone. Do promise to be there for each other if things get confusing or scary, and make a pact to pray for each other always. You're off to a great sisterhood start!

Your Mini-Woman Kit, Part 1

We're going to talk a lot in this section about being prepared for what's ahead. This project—which you'll add to at the end of each chapter in "Body Talk"—will give you a way to do some of that. Besides, it's fun, and who says this whole thing has to be so hard?

What you're doing:

You're creating a box that will become a storage place for some of the things you'll need on the puberty path. I'm calling it your *Mini-Woman Kit*, but you can think of it however you want to. Remember, though, that it isn't a "survival kit." You're going to do more than "survive" puberty. You're going to let it be wonderful.

What you'll need:

○ Any sturdy box that will fit into your underwear drawer or other private place (that is brother-free). It should have a lid.

○ Some kind of paper to cover it (so that you can remove the lid). That can be wrapping, craft, construction, or any paper that really looks like you. Plain white also works, as you'll see.

○ Art supplies you have around the house. Anything you want to draw, color, and/or write with, as well as glue or stick-on. Whatever you need to decorate your kit so that anyone looking at it would say, "Oh, that's *her* box."

How to make it happen:

1. Cover and design your box with as much imagination as you want.

2. Find a private place for it, the best choice for most girls being the undies drawer.

3. Be ready to fill it with some wonderful things as we continue our puberty path together. You ready, mini-woman?

That's What I'm Talkin' About

At the end of each chapter you'll also find this feature, which gives you a chance to journal or draw or simply think about how all you've just read applies to you. You can either fill in your answers here, or you can write/draw them in a special notebook. Here are this chapter's things to ponder when it's just you and God talkin':

I really want to invite these girls into the sisterhood:

_____

_____.

What I want to talk to them about (that I'm still shy about) is _____

_____

_____.

Puberty would be easier if _____

_____

_____.

The most confusing thing about it so far is _____

_____

_____.

The scariest thing so far is _____

_____

_____ .

The most surprising thing so far is _____

_____

_____ .

Already I feel better about _____

_____

_____ .

3

Bras, Breasts, and Other Girl Things

I can't think of a better way to start this chapter than with a story told by one of your fellow mini-women, in her own words:

> I'm the oldest in my family of three girls, so I was the first to get a bra. That day my grandma was with us when we were shopping, and she and my next youngest sister went to look at dresses. My mom said it was a good time for us to go look at bras for me. My youngest sister was in the cart playing with something, so I kind of forgot she was there.

"But when my mom put the bra in the cart, my little sister yelled (and I mean yelled), 'WHO'S GETTING THE BIKINI?!?!?!'

"I was like, 'Shh! It's not a bikini; it's a bra.'

"So then she said just as loudly as before, 'WELL, THEN, WHO'S GETTING THE BRA?!?!?!?'

"I flushed with embarrassment and whispered, 'I'm getting it. Shhh!'

"Her eyes got all big, and she stared at my chest for a moment, and then whispered super loudly, 'You're getting a BRA?'

"It was so embarrassing then. But now? I tell the story at every sleepover!"

That kind of says it all, doesn't it? Getting your first bra really is a big deal—and if it isn't to you, it apparently is to everybody else! Maybe that's because developing breasts is one of the first signs that you've started puberty *and* it's the one that's most obvious to other people. It can open you up to teasing (particularly from absurd little creep boys who don't know what to make of them), but also to the realization that you really are turning into a young woman—both at the same time.

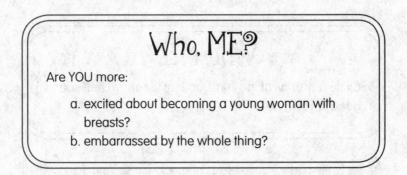

Who, ME?

Are YOU more:

    a. excited about becoming a young woman with breasts?

    b. embarrassed by the whole thing?

Since it *is* that first big puberty thing, it's a good place to begin as we walk this path together. Let's get our facts straight by answering some of the questions tween girls like you ask me.

HERE'S THE DEAL WITH BREASTS

> **"** I don't see what's so great about having breasts right now. **"**

You don't exactly have a choice about *having* breasts, but you *can* choose to be happy they're there. Developing breasts means:

- You're getting a new, feminine shape; it's a nice change.

- You can wear a different style of clothes; that's another nice change.

- You get to feel more grown-up.

- You *look* more grown-up, so anybody who knows anything will treat you less like a little girl who doesn't know anything.

> I get teased about my, y'know, chest, and I hate that. Even if I wear big shirts, people still make comments or stare.

Yeah, there are challenges that come with those breasts:

- Some people, especially boys, may tease you because your new body means things are changing in their world too, and that makes them nervous. (They can never just *act* nervous; they have to make it all about you, right?)

- You might feel like you're developing way ahead of the other girls or way behind them, and it seems like you're kind of unconnected at times.

Just So You Know

Breast development can start as early as eight years old or as late as thirteen years old. That's a wide range of "normal"!

- You may wonder if your breasts are normal, and it's

hard to know since you don't actually see a lot of other girls' breasts to compare yours to.

- You could have bra issues, like what size bra to wear, what style to pick, or how to get your mom to agree you need one.

- Your growing breasts might actually scare you because you still feel pretty young, and you don't think you're ready to be a woman yet.

Who, ME?

Put a check next to any of the items in the list above that YOU can relate to. Or circle them. (It's okay if you circle ALL of them; that's why you're reading this book, right?)

We'll take a look at all those breast challenges so you can enjoy this part of becoming a mini-woman. Let's start with what God has to say about blossoming chests.

GOT GOD?

Whenever I put God and breasts together in the same sentence, mini-women look at me and say, *"Okay, seriously. God thinks about THAT?"*

Uh, yeah. God created them, after all. As far as we can tell, God gave women breasts for a couple of reasons:

- God sculpted women to be attractive to men so the guys would want to marry them and live their lives with them. No guy who is worth being with ever got married just because he thought his wife's breasts were kinda cute. You are not your bra size! But your breasts are definitely a part of what makes you womanly and unique, no matter what size and shape they are.

• God also gave breasts a practical purpose, which was to feed babies. Your breasts contain mammary glands, which produce milk when a baby is born. Not all women will have children or breastfeed them if they do, but the right stuff is there just in case. God actually made it pretty easy for moms, when you think about it. No matter where they are, the milk is always there for their hungry infants.

As beautiful and functional as God makes breasts, he also instructs us to keep them safely tucked into our clothes unless we're in private with our husbands (or a doctor when necessary). That just shows you how precious breasts are. So feel free to thank God for this new shape your body is taking, and ask him to guide you in everything regarding it. Then you'll be ready to face the challenges, one by one.

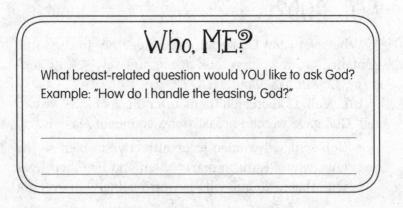

Who, ME?

What breast-related question would YOU like to ask God? Example: "How do I handle the teasing, God?"

_____

_____

That Is SO Me!

Okay, on to you. This quiz will help you see that you're right where you need to be breast-wise. Put a star next to the description that sounds most like you. You'll need to know two definitions first.

- nipple: the raised nub in the center of your breast

- areola: the colored circle around your nipple

1. My chest is still flat, and my nipples are a little raised.

2. A small, flat breast bud has formed under my nipple, sort of like a button. The areola is a little wider than it used to be.

3. I actually have a small breast, not just a bud. My areolas stand out now.

4. My areolas and nipples have formed a separate little mound on my breast. They're pointier than they used to be.

5. My areolas and nipples aren't a separate mound. Everything is one smooth breast.

The description you drew a star by tells what stage of breast development you're in. It'll help you see for sure that where you are is absolutely normal.

Stage 1—*Pre-puberty*: No breasts yet, but you'll get them when your body's ready. You're not "behind." You're simply you.

Stage 2—*Breast Buds*: These quarter-sized bumps are the very beginning of your future breasts. Don't worry if they aren't exactly the same size or they stay this way for a year or they blossom into the next stage after a few months. It's all good.

Stage 3—*Developing Breasts*: The shape of your breasts now is a lot like they'll be when you're an adult, only smaller. No worries. Enjoy wearing the cutest, most comfortable bra you can find (more on that later).

Stage 4—*Nipple and Areola Mound*: This is an interesting stage because your breasts may stay the way they are in shape and just grow larger, or they might move on to the next stage. Have I mentioned that everybody's different?

Stage 5—*Adult Breasts*: Even though you aren't an adult yet, your breasts have fully developed. They might continue to grow in size, but their shape is a sign of your womanly self—and they're fabulous.

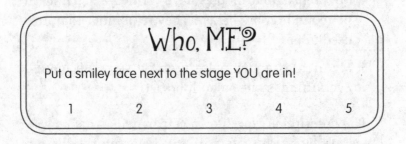

Who, ME?

Put a smiley face next to the stage YOU are in!

| 1 | 2 | 3 | 4 | 5 |

HERE'S THE DEAL WITH BREAST "SURPRISES"

Mini-women tell me that some things happen while their breasts are developing that they didn't exactly expect. Just in case you experience some of those too …

" Sometimes my breasts hurt. Is that, like, normal? "

Yeah, as breasts grow from stage to stage, they can be itchy or tender or even painful. That's normal (bummer, huh?), but just like all growing pains, these will go away. If the soreness really bothers you, ask your mom if you can take some ibuprofen.

Who, ME?

What's the most surprising thing YOU have experienced with your budding breasts?

- **"There's this weird bumpy thing under my nipple. Could that be cancer or something?"** A bump under the nipple when the breast is growing is not breast cancer. It's just part of the blooming process.

- **One of my breasts is bigger than the other, and it kind of freaks me out.** Your breasts won't necessarily grow at the same rate. Don't worry if one's smaller than the other. They'll even out, although no woman's breasts are identical to each other. The difference is usually too tiny to even notice.

- **Is it abnormal that my nipples sort of go in instead of out?** Some girls' nipples don't stick out, but seem to sink in. Not to worry if yours are inverted like that. In case you've actually wondered about it, you'll still be able to breastfeed a baby.

- **I haven't told my mom this, but sometimes my breasts leak. Is that okay?** A little occasional fluid out of your breasts is not unusual. The hormones are just doing their thing. Don't try to squeeze anything out, though. It just makes your breasts leakier.

HERE'S THE DEAL ABOUT BRAS

Once your breasts appear, you'll probably start thinking about a bra. It seems like there's a lot to consider, so here are the answers to the bra questions most girls ask.

> ❝At first I would wiggle and scrunch around. Everyone must have guessed I was wearing a bra for the first time!❞

Just So You Know

Until the 1920s, women actually referred to their undergarments as unmentionables!

"When should I start wearing a bra?" There's really no "should" about it, but these are the main reasons for wearing a bra:

- If your breasts jiggle when you're active.

- If your breasts are sore, the support helps.

- If you don't like your nipples showing through your clothes.

- If everybody else your age is wearing them and you just want to be like the group.

Who, ME?

Do any of those reasons for wearing a bra apply to YOU?

There's nothing wrong with any of those reasons (even the last one). This is a time of change in your life, and if a bra makes it easier and more comfortable, then absolutely, you should wear one. You'll know when you're ready.

> "Around my tenth birthday my breasts were beginning to show, though not that much, but I really, really, REALLY wanted a bra cuz everyone else had one. I kept begging until, for my birthday, I got three sports bras. I have them to this day, even though they don't fit anymore, because it was so cool."

What if my mom says I don't need one yet, but I think I do? Show your mom the answer to the question on the previous page. If she needs more convincing, be your most mature self and explain exactly why you're craving a little lingerie. If she still says no, try wearing a pretty cami or a tank top instead, and ask her again in a month or so. If you don't nag, pout, or pitch a fit, she'll respect your maturity and may decide you're ready for this step after all. Keep in mind that it's sometimes hard for moms to let their daughters grow up, so go easy on her.

> "My mom just said, 'Do you want to get a bra?' and I said, 'Sure.' No big deal."

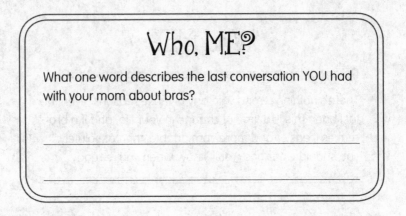

Who, ME?

What one word describes the last conversation YOU had with your mom about bras?

_____

_____

"*My breasts are big enough for a bra, but I DON'T want to wear one. They look so uncomfortable!*" Okay, yeah, wearing a bra takes a little getting used to, but it doesn't have to be all tight and restrictive. A lot of girls, especially really active ones, start with a sports bra, which has no hooks or underwires.

> 66 At first I was so mad I had to wear a bra. But I've been wearing one for a really long time now, and I don't even think about it anymore. 99

"*How do I know what size to wear? I don't get the numbers and letters thing.*" Bras come in sizes like 32A, 34C, and 36B. The number is about the measurement around your chest, called the **band size**. The letter tells the size of your actual breast, called the **cup size**.

Here's how to figure out yours, using a tape measure while you're wearing no shirt or a very thin, close-fitting top. The blanks are here for you to fill in.

- Measure in inches around your rib cage right under your breasts: _____ inches

- Add 5 to that number: _____ inches. If this number is odd, add another 1. That's your **band size**: _____

- Measure around your body at your breasts, putting the tape measure at nipple level. That's your **chest plus breast size**: _____

Just So You Know

It's important to wear the right size bra because:

- If the band size is too small, it'll feel tight and uncomfortable.

- If the band size is too loose, it will ride up on your breasts.

- If the cup size is too small, it'll squish your breasts out under your armpits!

- If the cup size is too big, your bra will wrinkle and pucker and look funky under your clothes.

"When I was getting a bra for the first time, I was so embarrassed about getting measured up, and I was afraid somebody I knew was going to be there and see me looking at the bras. But everything turned out fine. It's funny how much you worry and make a huge deal of a thing in your head, and then once you've done it, it's not so big after all. **"**

Now you can figure out your cup size:

- If band size is larger than chest-plus-breast size: AAA

- Measurements are equal: AA

- Band size is up to 1 inch smaller: A

- Band size is up to 2 inches smaller: B

- Band size is up to 3 inches smaller: C

- Band size is up to 4 inches smaller: D

- Band size is up to 5 inches smaller: DD

Put your band size next to your cup size and, voilà! you have your bra size (like 30AA, 36B, etc.). Always try on a bra, though, because the style can make a difference in how it fits.

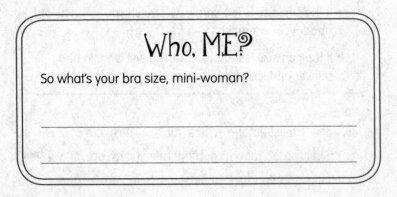

Who, ME?

So what's your bra size, mini-woman?

_____

_____

"Who knew there were so many kinds of bras? Help!" It can seem confusing, but basically we're talking six styles. See if this helps:

> **"** I think the perfect bra is one that isn't hot and doesn't squeeze. **"**

Training—This light bra, which comes in small, medium, and large, can help you get used to wearing a bra or make you feel feminine (even if you barely have breast buds). It won't "train" your breasts to be bigger, smaller, or perkier, so if you don't want to wear one, that's perfectly okay.

Just So You Know

Training bras used to be called "bralettes." How funny is that?!

Soft Cup—This very comfortable bra is seamless and smooth and light. It lets your breasts look natural. If you feel "saggy" in a soft-cup bra or seem to be spilling out of it, you might need a bra with more support.

Just So You Know

If you tend to sweat a lot, an all-cotton bra is a good choice. Less chance of getting a rash.

Underwire—Just like it sounds, this bra has a wire encased in soft fabric just below each breast. It keeps your breasts snug and lifted and doesn't let them bounce. It isn't uncomfortable when it fits right.

> I hate itchy bras.

Push-Up—This is for girls with smaller breasts who want extra lift and shape. At this point in your life, a push-up bra is probably too sophisticated.

Sports—Whether you play sports or you're always on the move ... or you just have to be comfortable or you get cranky, a sports bra is for you. It's like a very tight tank top cut off just below your breasts. It does flatten you out, but who cares?

> One time I put my sports bra on and it felt weird. Then it was gym, and when I was changing my top, the girls kinda looked at me strange. I wondered why, and then I got home and realized it was on backwards!

Minimizer—If you should happen to have breasts no one else has caught up to yet (C cup or above) and you feel self-conscious, it's perfectly okay to choose a minimizer bra. It's designed to make breasts look smaller without flattening them out. Be prepared for the straps to be thick, and if you're way active, be sure you can really move with this bra on.

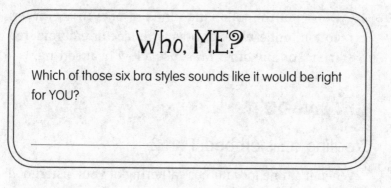

Who, ME?

Which of those six bra styles sounds like it would be right for YOU?

_____

" The perfect bra would be an invisible one that you couldn't feel, but it was there. "

"Do I have to wash a bra some special way?" If you don't want your bra to fall apart or become like a piece of cooked pasta, you'll need to treat it with care. Even if your mom does the laundry, it doesn't hurt to take responsibility for your "foundation garments." (How funny is that old-fashioned name for bras?)

- To keep the elastic from wearing out, don't wear the same bra more than two days in a row.

- Your bra will need to be washed as soon as it has the first sign of sweat stains or body smell.

- Washing by hand in lukewarm water with a gentle detergent is best. If you do toss it into the washer, put it in a mesh lingerie bag and wash at the coolest setting on a delicate cycle.

- Never use chlorine bleach, or bye-bye elastic!

- Don't put the following kinds of bras in the dryer: cotton, underwire, or bras with lace or embroidered trim. For any other bras, use a low heat setting.

YOU CAN DO IT

Creating a Sisterhood, Part 2

When it's time for another gathering of your sisterhood in the usual no-boys-allowed place, here are some bra- and breast-centered things you can do together.

1. Review the ground rules you established last time. The MOST important thing is to make sure everybody feels comfortable enough to talk about anything she wants.

2. You can use "Who, ME?" sections to get the conversation going. Fun stuff!

3. Together, design the perfect bra. What would it look, feel ... even smell like?

4. Speaking of smells, if you're a bunch who enjoy crafts, you can each make a sachet to help keep bras smelling fresh in the undies drawer. (You can also do this by yourself, of course.)

What you'll need for each girl (or have her bring):

○ a 5" x 5" square of fabric that's cotton, a cotton blend, or lace—something that won't block the scent of potpourri (like a big ol' hunk of wool!)

○ a piece of ribbon or string about 6 inches long

○ ¼ cup of potpourri—dried cinnamon sticks, whole cloves, dried citrus peel, or dried rose petals

How to make it happen:

1. Put the small square of fabric on a table or counter, pretty side down.

2. Put the potpourri, or dried goods, in the center of it.

3. Gather all four corners together to form a little sack.

4. Tie it closed with the ribbon or string.

Placed among your undies, it'll keep the whole drawer smelling amazing.

Your Mini-Woman Kit, Part 2

What you're doing:

Whether you're an ultrafeminine princess, an on-the-go athlete, or somebody in between, it's important to feel like the girl you are, right down to your undies. You can start now by creating a special space for your "unmentionables." Whatever you call your bras, panties, socks, camisoles, and anything else you wear under your clothes, have some fun making your collection special.

What you'll need:

○ all your undergarments (clean, of course!)

○ the drawer you keep them in

○ a piece of very YOU fabric to line it with (pink satin? wild print? cute plaid?)

How to make it happen:

1. Take everything out of the drawer, and set it aside.

2. Clean your drawer as necessary: Vacuum it or wipe it out with a damp cloth. Even spray it with a fabric freshener if you need to.

3. Spread your YOU fabric out in the bottom of your drawer.

4. Organize all your undies into piles—bras, panties, camis, tights, socks.

5. Fold each item in each pile, and give the pile its own space in your drawer. Don't forget to leave room for your Mini-Woman Kit in there. If you're using a big drawer, you can even make dividers out of cardboard and place them under the fabric first.

6. Tuck in that sachet you made, and you have the perfect uniquely YOU place for those mini-woman additions to your undies collection—and you'll always be able to find what you need!

That's What I'm Talkin' About

Here's your chance again to journal, draw, or simply think about how all you've just read applies to you. As always, you can either fill in your answers here or you can write/draw them in a special notebook.

Things to ponder when it's just you and God talkin':

As I think about my breast development, I still wonder ___

_____

_____.

Right now, my attitude about bras is _____

_____

_____.

I could use some help with _____

_____

_____.

What I'm most grateful for in my mini-womaness is _____

_____

_____.

4

Every MONTH?

When I ask tween girls, "What freaks you out the most about puberty?" they are *not* shy about telling me.

> My mom said we had to talk about me getting my period, so we read a book together. I was grossed out.

> I've had my period a couple of times, but it will never come on schedule, and once I got it at my friend's sleepover, and none of my friends knew about periods, so it was hard.

> **"** I hate periods cuz I could bawl and cry my head off when somebody sneezes, or collapse into laughing seizures when the tiniest thing happens.**"**

You've probably heard horror stories like that yourself or even told a few! That's kind of a bummer because getting your first period doesn't have to be, well, horrible. *Other* mini-women will tell you:

> **"** To all of you who haven't gotten your period yet: It's annoying, but it really isn't that bad. You get used to it.**"**

That's reassuring, right? I think we can do even better than that, though. I think we can get you so informed and prepared, the whole period thing can actually be a celebration of your mini-woman-ness. Not the party hats and ice cream kind of celebration, but … well, you'll see. Let's get some facts straight first.

Who, ME?

Right now, are you more on the "horror story" side or the "not so bad" side?

_____

HERE'S THE DEAL ABOUT PERIOD BASICS

The real word for "getting your period" is *menstruation*.

- *What you're going to see when you start menstruating* is a fluid that looks like blood coming out of your vagina and onto your panties or a piece of toilet paper. There may be from a quarter to a third of a cup of fluid over the course of three to seven days every month.

- *The reason some girls get freaked out about it* is because they have to keep that fluid from getting on their clothes (chairs, couches, beds, car seats … you get the idea). If that does happen, yeah, it can be embarrassing. Anything new seems like a huge thing at first, but once you get used to wearing protection for those few days, it just becomes part of being a girl.

The first question tween girls usually ask when they find out about periods is:

Why do we have to go through something that's so messy and embarrassing? What's the point in it?

Menstruation is part of the system in you that can produce babies—your **reproductive system**. Take a look at this diagram of a female's body:

Here's how all of that works:

- The **ovaries**, those little almond-shaped organs, hold the eggs (also called **ova**) that you were born with. There are about 400,000 of them in there, some of which could help make babies someday. (Though not 400,000 of them!) The ovaries also make the hormones estrogen and progesterone that kick in at puberty (remember those from chapter 1?) and tell your ovaries to release an egg. One ovary lets one egg go one month; the other ovary lets an egg go the next month. That's called **ovulation**, and it happens about two weeks before your period. You might even feel some twinges at that time.

- The **fallopian tube** (you have two), which curves around and sort of reaches for an ovary, catches the egg as it's released from the ovary. It's only about as thick as a needle, so you can imagine how tiny the egg is. The fan-shaped part just over the ovary has fringe called **fimbria** that push the egg toward the tube, where it's pushed along by little hairs on its way to the uterus. That trip takes about four days. If a guy's sperm entered the scene right about then, and it met the egg and broke through its outer shell, that would be the beginning of a baby.

- The **uterus**, the pear-shaped organ, is also called the *womb*. Your fist is about the size of your uterus. That's where an egg fertilized by a sperm (described above) would nestle and grow into a baby. The walls of the uterus are made of strong, stretchy muscle, so it can grow bigger when a mom is pregnant. Right after the egg is released from the ovary, estrogen tells the uterus to start building a lining of tissue and some new blood vessels to nurture the unborn baby. But if the egg isn't fertilized by a sperm (no baby), all that tissue and blood built up on the inside walls of the uterus have to be flushed out. Ta da! There's your period.

- That small opening at the bottom of the uterus is the **cervix**. It opens to release the fluid of your period or to allow a baby to come out when it's born.

- Both emerge from the same place, the **vagina**, that four- or five-inch-long passage from the outside to the inside of your body. Don't freak—it expands a *lot* for a baby to be born. God has all of that taken care of.

Who, ME?

Close your eyes and see if you can imagine all of that going on inside YOU right now. Pretty cool, huh?

Some more questions mini-women like you ask:

What does a period look like? I mean, is it going to be like I'm bleeding to death?

Your period's made up of three things:

1. The tissue that would have been the baby-holding lining that you don't need if there's no baby; this can look like red clumps.

2. Some mucus from your cervix and vagina.

3. Some blood; that gives your period flow a red color, but it isn't all blood, so not to worry. It might be brownish at the beginning and go to darker red, and then maybe back to brownish before it stops. The heaviest part of your period will be the first day or

two, and then it will gradually taper off. It will never "gush out of you" like a garden hose!

How long is your period supposed to last? What's normal?

Ah, there's that word *normal* again. Let's call "normal" between three and seven days. If yours is longer, ask your mom how long hers usually are. If eight days is the usual for her, then it makes sense that it would be the same for you. For any longer than that, Mom should probably consult a doctor.

What do I do with all that stuff coming out of me?

That's where **feminine hygiene products** come in. (That's what they call them in the grocery store or drugstore.) It's much simpler than picking out a bra because you only have two basic choices.

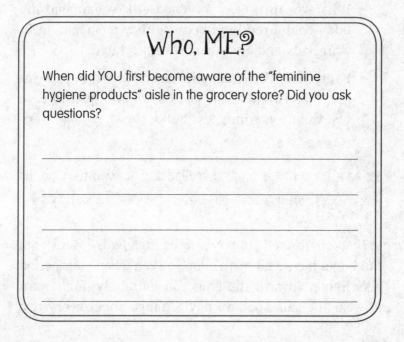

Who, ME?

When did YOU first become aware of the "feminine hygiene products" aisle in the grocery store? Did you ask questions?

_____

_____

_____

_____

_____

Pads—Because they're so easy to use, most girls start with these. A pad's made of several layers of soft cotton in the shape of a dainty pillow. It has a sticky strip, so all you have to do is peel off the paper, press the pad into the crotch of your underwear, and it absorbs fluid. It feels bulky at first, but nobody can see it and you do get used to it. There are different kinds of pads, but we'll keep it simple:

- **Maxi pads** are super thick in case you need a lot of coverage the first few days. Then you can switch to **regular** (thinner) pads.

- Pads with **wings** wrap around the edges of your panties so you don't get side leaks. That can make you feel extra secure.

- Whatever thickness you choose, I recommend the **body-contoured** kind because they're shaped to fit your body and are the most comfortable.

- **Panty liners or panty shields** are very thin pads for the lighter flow of the last day or two, just in case you want something less bulky.

> **"**If your pad is slipping around and soaking through the sides, wear pads with wings. They're the best.**"**

How often am I supposed to change pads? Menstrual fluid does have a bit of an odor, so even when your period gets lighter toward the end, you definitely don't want to wear the same pad all day! Change about every two hours for the first half of your period and every four to five hours the second half. Most pads and liners come individually wrapped so you can pop some in your purse or backpack. Be sure you have enough so you can change as often as you need to. (More on that later.)

Just So You Know

There are pads and panty liners sized just right for tweens, and they come in cute glittery boxes, with colors and patterns on the pads themselves!

What do I do with the used pad when I take it off? (This just all seems so icky!) You definitely don't want to flush a pad down the toilet because it'll clog the plumbing. Just fold it or roll it into a ball, wrap it in toilet paper or the wrapper many pads come in, and tuck it into the trash can. Most public restrooms have a metal container in each stall just for that purpose. If you're embarrassed about crossing a public restroom to toss your wrapped-up pad in the trash, just remember that (a) every woman has the same experience and (b) the less freaked out you act, the less attention you'll draw to that simple matter of throwing something away. Oh, and really, it isn't icky. It's just hygiene, like brushing your teeth or putting on deodorant.

Who, ME?

Next time you're in the girls' restroom at school or church, check out the situation as if you'd just started your period. Would it be easy to handle, or does that room need some help?

_____

_____

_____

Tampons—A tampon is a tube-shaped narrow strip of cotton that you insert into your vagina, where it absorbs the fluid before it even leaves your body. Since your vagina is muscular and flexible, it molds around the tampon to keep it from falling out. When you're ready to remove it, you just tug on the string that's left hanging outside your vagina, and it slides right out. A lot of girls and women like to use a tampon because …

- You can't even feel it if it's inserted right.

- It doesn't take up much room in your purse, backpack, or even your pocket.

- You won't have odor issues.

- No one will be able to see it, even with a swimsuit or gymnastics or dance clothes.

Not everybody uses them, especially in the early months or years of having periods, because …

- The vaginal opening is small when you're young, so a tampon can be hard for some girls to put in.

- It takes some practice to insert one, and if you're already trying to adjust to having periods in the first place, it's less frustrating to wait a while.

- Some moms don't approve of them for girls your age.

I want to try tampons, and my mom won't even discuss it. What's that about?

Of course, if Mom says no, you really have to respect that decision. If you do want to talk to her about it, this might help. These are the main reasons moms don't allow tampons and some information that might put her mind at rest. (Or you could just wait a while. Mom has to get used to you growing up too.)

- "You might get sick." She's probably thinking about a rare condition called toxic-shock syndrome, which usually only occurs when women don't change their tampons regularly.

- "You'll have worse cramps." Actually, cramps aren't caused by tampons. We'll talk more about what does make your stomach hurt during your period.

- "Tampons are only for married women." Physically, it doesn't make any difference whether you're married or not; tampons are safe for most women.

So if my mom says it's okay to try a tampon, how do I use it?

First, choose the kind of tampon you think will be best for you.

- **Cardboard applicator**—Made up of two cardboard tubes, one inside the other; the outer one slides the tampon in, and the inner one pushes the tampon into place. They may get a little beat-up in your purse or backpack unless you keep them in a special plastic holder.

- **Plastic applicator**—This works the same way as cardboard and holds up better. It's also smoother than cardboard, but not as safe for the environment when you throw it away.

- **No applicator**—This tampon is so small you can just push it in with your finger; good choice for beginners—no moving parts! (And, again, it isn't "icky"; this is your own body, and there's nothing disgusting about it.)

> **❝** I got my first period when I was in Florida, and I couldn't go swimming because I could NOT figure out tampons! **❞**

Like pads, tampons come in different thicknesses (called **absorbencies**). It's good to have an assortment so you can use the appropriate absorbency for any point in your period. They come in **extra absorbent**, **super**, **regular**, **slender**, and **junior**. As you get to know your own periods, you'll find out what combination you need. You may use super the first two days, regular the next two, and slender for the rest of the time, or extra absorbent the whole time—or some other combination.

1. Read all the directions on the box before you start, and if you have any questions, ask for help from your mom, big sister, or another adult woman you trust. Then relax and take it step by step. If the tampon won't slide in easily, try again later. It isn't a failure if it doesn't work out the first time. A lot of girls are in high school before they've grown enough to use a tampon.

2. These are the usual things that trip girls up when they're trying a tampon for the first time:

- Aiming the tampon straight up instead of at a slant; your vagina angles toward the small of your back; who knew, right?

- Vagina is too dry; try some petroleum jelly on it, but nothing with a scent, which could irritate your skin.

- Not holding the folds of skin open (those are called **labia**); you might just be pushing the tampon against skin.

- Tampon is too big; try a smaller size or just wait until you grow a little. There's plenty of time, because you'll probably have periods until you're in your forties or fifties!

- It goes in but it hurts, which means it isn't in far enough. Push gently or start over with a fresh one.

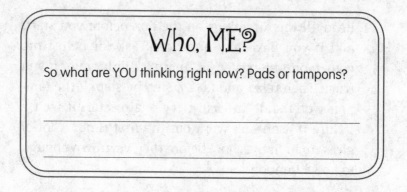

Who, ME?

So what are YOU thinking right now? Pads or tampons?

_____

_____

So do I just keep all this stuff around all the time? I mean, who knows when my first period's going to surprise me?

To answer that question, let's turn to our quiz.

That Is SO Me!

These are all signs that a period will start in the near future. Circle the ones that are happening to you. (And remember, everyone's body is on a different timetable, so don't moan if you don't circle any. Your day will come!) BTW, if you are brother-challenged, you can keep track on a separate piece of paper.

○ My stomach area is puffy and bloated.

○ I'm older than eight.

○ I'm in breast stage three.

○ It's been about two years since I developed pubic hair.

○ Sometimes I see white sticky stuff in my underwear.

○ I have the munchies.

○ My breasts are tender and a little puffier than they were at first.

○ I have a lower backache.

○ I'm crankier or weepier than usual.

○ I'm tired and kind of sluggish.

○ I suddenly have pimples!

If you circled at least **five** of the eleven signs, you'll want to be prepared with supplies at home and in your backpack or purse. There's no way to tell if your period will happen tomorrow or more than a month from now, but you'll feel more secure if you have it together. Besides, who knows when a friend will be caught padless? We girls are all in this together.

Just So You Know

Girls often start menstruating at approximately the same age their mothers or grandmothers did.

HERE'S THE DEAL ABOUT PERIOD MYTHS

You'll probably hear a lot of things about periods that just aren't true. These are some of the common whoppers:

- *"Menstrual blood is poisonous."* No way. It's made by your own body!

- *"A boy can tell by smelling your breath that you're on your period."* What? No, he cannot.

- *"A dentist can tell you're on your period."* Nah. And besides, if he or she could, who cares? This is a professional person who isn't going to announce it in the waiting room.

- *"You can't go swimming if you're on your period."* Why not if you're wearing a tampon? Now, a pad would be a problem because it's like a sponge …

- *"A tampon can get lost up in your body."* Not gonna happen. The only place it could go would be through your cervix into your uterus, and the opening of the cervix is about the size of a match head!

- *"You shouldn't wash your hair when you're on your period."* Actually, there's no *better* time to stay clean and looking your best. It'll make you feel better on bloated days.

Just remember: If you can do it when you're *not* on your period, you can do it *during* your period. After all, it isn't an illness—it's normal!

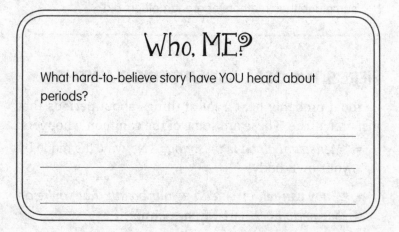

Who, ME?

What hard-to-believe story have YOU heard about periods?

> **When I have my period, I try to go outside and ride my bike because it helps my cramps a LOT!**

Just So You Know

In case you're interested, cramps are caused by **prostaglandin**, a chemical in the body that makes the smooth muscle in the uterus contract. Those contractions, or "cramps," can be dull, sharp, or even kind of intense. The good news is that they aren't constant, and they usually last only a few days.

> **When I'm getting ready to have my period, I have random mood swings, I get pimples, and I get a really sore tummy. But once it starts, I actually feel better. And afterwards? That's the best.**

> **Whenever I have my period, I turn into some irritable, emotional, snappy freak and become totally defensive and put up a wall toward everyone. But at the same time, when I'm acting all tough, I feel really weak and puny and like running to my room to cry.**

> **I REALLY need tips on how to control my temper when I have PMS!**

HERE'S THE DEAL ON PERIOD PROBLEMS

So far I've made having your period sound pretty easy, and it is most of the time. The few things that can bum you out are usually simple to fix.

Cramps — Cramps are caused by the tightening of the uterus muscles. Some girls get them before and during their periods, and some don't. If you do get them, you're usually talking about a mild, uncomfortable lower stomachache, but one out of ten girls gets sharp pain that makes her want to curl up in a ball for the day, and she may even have some vomiting and diarrhea. Other girls never have any discomfort at all. (Lucky!) If you're one of the unfortunate ones, this should help:

- *Put some heat on your tummy*—a heating pad, an herb pack you put in the microwave, or anything warm that will help your muscles relax.

- *Do some gentle stretches,* like reaching down to touch your toes or sitting on your heels and lowering your forehead to the floor with your arms stretched out on the floor in front of you.

- *Be sure to get to bed on time, eat healthy* (see chapter 6), *and drink plenty of water* (not soda).

- *If all of that doesn't help, ask your mom for a mild pain reliever like ibuprofen* (not aspirin). Ask to see a doctor for severe cramps that interfere with your activities. Your period doesn't have to be a time of suffering.

PMS—When a girl is crabby or snappy, you hear people—even guys—joking about PMS. Like everybody (including them) doesn't get like that once in a while!

Real PMS stands for *premenstrual syndrome*, and it's a combination of symptoms that affect some girls the week before their period. It can include:

- Feeling (and being) puffy and bloated.

- Wanting to eat everything that isn't nailed down, especially sweets and *really* especially chocolate.

- Being crabby and irritable or feeling on the verge of tears every minute.

- Ready to hug anybody (even your brother) one minute and ready to smack those same people (especially your brother) the next.

- Needing to take a nap an hour after you just got up from one.

Although not everybody experiences PMS, the symptoms are real. They are *not* your imagination. PMS is caused by the drop in estrogen just before your period. Estrogen makes you feel happy, so when it isn't there, you're likely to feel down—physically and emotionally. However, PMS doesn't mean you get to be the Wicked Witch of the West and everybody else just has to deal with you. There are things you can do to help yourself be easier to live with:

- *Get some fun exercise.*

- *Eat healthy carbs for snacks* before your period and for the first few days. (See chapter 6 for ideas.)

- *Don't eat much sugar or drink caffeine.*

- *Do eat lots of veggies, whole grains, and nuts.*

- *Get at least eight hours of sleep a night. Nine is even better.*

- *Talk to somebody who will understand about your feelings.*

- *You might also try spending some time alone or doing quiet things.* (Just don't scream at everyone who knocks on your door ...)

- *Be nice to yourself during your alone time.* Hot bubble bath? Soft music while you read your favorite book? Curl up with your cat? Just remember that being nice to yourself doesn't mean eating a whole package of Oreos.

Bloating—Feeling like the Pillsbury Doughboy? That puffy look and feel in your lower abdomen is your body holding on to fluid. You might even feel like an inflatable toy in your face, fingers, breasts, and feet. It will go away once your period starts, but in the meantime, here are some things you can do:

- *Get some exercise.*

- *Cut back on salt and salty foods* (yeah, that's right, chips, fries ...), especially two weeks before your period.

- *Eat meat, fish, poultry, whole grains, and leafy green veggies instead of* junk food, fast food, and soda.

- *Drink at least six glasses of water a day* to flush out the fluid your body is hoarding like treasure.

- *For bloated breasts, try a sports bra or other snug bra* to make them less tender.

Irregular periods—Period one month, none for the next two, then two a month can be annoying, but that isn't unusual in the first two or three years. That's because your body is still adjusting to those new hormones; it won't be this way forever, I promise! Keep supplies handy all the time until things settle into a regular rhythm, which is usually a period every twenty-one to thirty-five days. You keep track of your periods from the beginning of one to the beginning of the next one. There are other causes of irregular periods, but here are some things that can cause your body to get out of balance (and some suggestions to keep it in balance):

- *Eating a lot of junk food (or not enough veggies and good protein) or going on fad diets.* When you read the "Table Talk" chapter, you'll get some ideas for how to avoid that.

- *Moving or visiting a new place.* Give yourself a chance to adjust slowly. It's okay if you don't feel right at home the first day.

- *Gaining or losing weight too fast.* Eating right helps there. If your doctor says you need to lose weight for your health, take it "slow and healthy." No lose-twenty-pounds-this-weekend diets!

- *Being upset.* Since that can be part of being a tween in the first place, even without your period, talk out your issues with an adult you trust. Write in a journal about stuff that bothers you. Be sure you have enough downtime to play, daydream, and just veg. Don't let resentments build up, and be sure to go to God with everything.

- *Being sick or getting hurt.* Just know that any kind of trauma to your body may affect your period. Simply concentrate on your healing. Things will right themselves again.

- *Getting too MUCH exercise.* Didn't think that was possible? If you're pushing yourself to the point of exhaustion on the playing field (and your diet isn't all that great) and your periods stop, your body is trying to tell you to back off some when you feel heavy fatigue or pain. Your body is still growing—it isn't ready for a marathon yet!

- *Not getting ANY exercise.* Couch potatoes often have whacky periods. Get up, and get moving. The "Confessions of a Couch Potato" chapter will help you with that.

Irregular periods are the ones that catch you off guard. If you start yours when there are no supplies available, don't panic. You can improvise:

- Use folded toilet paper, tissue, or paper towels to make a pad to slip into your underwear until you can get to the real thing.

- If you're in a public restroom, look for a coin-operated machine. No money? It's okay to ask that woman washing her hands if she has change. No woman wants a fellow female to be without the right stuff; we've all been there.

- If blood has gotten on your clothes, tie a sweater, jacket, or shirt around your waist and head for the nearest place to get a pad (school nurse's office, for example). If you have time, you can do the sweater-around-the-waist trick, take off your stained pants or skirt, wash it in cold water in the sink, and dry it with the hand blower.

- Don't spend a lot of time worrying that you're going to end up walking around with blood on your clothes, totally clueless unless somebody tells you. That doesn't usually happen. You'll probably feel something wet and sticky before it ever gets on your clothes. Most girls don't bleed enough right at first for it to seep through. Just keep a pad in your purse or backpack, pay attention to changes in the way you feel, and relax. If it does happen, you'll have a great story to tell at the next sleepover!

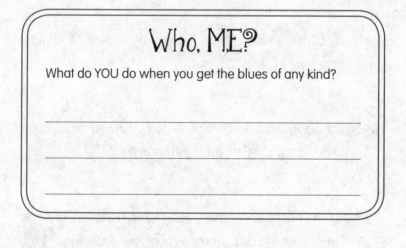

Who, ME?

What do YOU do when you get the blues of any kind?

_____

_____

_____

❝The most confusing thing about my period is that it's really random, even though I've had it for two years.

It always seems to come a week early or late. I was at a camp really far away from home, and near the start of the week my period came even though it wasn't due 'til two weeks away. Luckily one of my friends was there to help me ask the counselor for pads. But I had such bad cramps, I just started crying. THAT was the embarrassing part.

If your first period starts at school, stay calm. Don't freak, and if you have girlfriends, then you can tell them or ask a female teacher you trust to give you a pad. DO NOT be embarrassed; it's a thing all women go through.

Even if you don't feel comfortable talking to your mom about periods, according to your fellow mini-women, there are other options:

My older sisters have all been through it, and they help me.

My big sister and I share a room, and at night I ask her questions after the lights are out.

My mom was 3,000 miles away when I started my first period, but my dad got me through the whole thing.

Who, ME?

Whom have YOU talked to about periods? If nobody yet, whom would you like to get your info from and discuss your feelings with?

_____

_____

_____

GOT GOD?

You thought it was funky talking to God about breasts—but periods? Really?

Really.

Probably the reason God and menstruation don't seem to go together is because of Israelite traditions, some of which we can find in the Old Testament:

- Anybody who touched a woman when she was having her period was considered unclean until evening. (Leviticus 15:19)

- Anything she sat on or laid down on—anything she breathed on, practically—wasn't to be touched by anyone, or that would make them unclean. (Leviticus 19:20–23) You didn't want to be "unclean" in those days; it meant you had to stay away from anything sacred, like the temple, until you went through a ritual to be cleansed, which wasn't just a matter of washing your hands.

- Once a girl started having periods, no man except her husband could touch her again, ever, not even her father. She basically went hugless until she got married. (Israelite tradition)

You don't have to worry about being confined to the garage because you're "unclean" for seven days every month. Still, amid the cramps and the worrying about bleeding on your favorite jeans and the pads you're sick of by the fifth day, having periods can feel like somebody's cursing you. That must be why some women still call menstruation "the curse."

That's a bummer, because the whole period process is just part of the amazing system God created for the nurturing of babies before they're born. You're not thinking about being a mom anytime soon, but girls used to get married and have babies when they weren't much older than you are, so it probably made a lot more sense long ago to have periods at a young age.

It's hard for you, at eight or ten or twelve, to relate to that, so if you aren't going to let your period feel like a "curse," you'll need to work on having a pretty positive attitude. God understands that periods can be a bit of a nuisance (as in, pain in the neck!), but God obviously wants you to see that, overall, being a woman is a beautiful thing.

The Song of Songs, a very short book in the Old Testament, can help you with that. It's a love poem showing how much God loves you, just the way a groom loves his bride. You might not be able to relate to God saying your teeth are as beautiful as a flock of sheep and your cheeks are like two halves of a pomegranate, but you can certainly think of this verse when you're feeling "cursed." God says,

> "Arise, come, my darling;
> my beautiful one, come with me."

Song of Songs 2:13

It sort of makes the cramps and the bloating worth it, doesn't it?

● ●

YOU CAN DO IT

Creating a Sisterhood, Part 3

When it's time for another gathering of your sisterhood in the usual no-boys-allowed place, here are some "Yikes! Periods!" things you can do together.

1. Review the ground rules you've established and practiced. It's especially important when you get into this territory that each girl feels like she can say what she needs to say or not say anything at all.

2. Just like last time, you can use "Who, ME?" sections to get the conversation going. Be sure to have this book available for when questions come up or somebody states a "myth" like it's the gospel truth. Girl gatherings can be prime places for people to get confused unless you have the right information on hand.

3. Together, decide exactly how you're going to support each other if/when somebody gets her period at school (or any other place where you're all together, like camp, youth group, dance studio, soccer games or practices, etc.) Here are some things to consider:

- Where will supplies always be found?

- What will the signal be for "I just started. Help!" to use in case there are boys around. (Examples: Tugging on the left earlobe—your own, not your friend's! Giving the secret handshake. Using a code word.)

- Which teachers and other adults do you all agree would be helpful and discreet if you need them? They can be part of the sisterhood too.

- What promise will you make to each other that anything period-related will be handled with privacy and respect?

- How will you celebrate as each of you enters this part of mini-womanhood?

4. Make a list of the *good* things about this big move into adult-ness. Okay, so maybe the list will be short, but the first thing on it can be, "It brings us closer

together as friends because we need each other."
Then celebrate that. With chocolate.

Your Mini-Woman Kit, Part 3

What you're doing:

No matter where you are when it comes to periods, you can probably be more prepared than you are now, so let's make that part of your kit.

What you'll need:

◯ a large box of whatever feminine hygiene products you use or are going to use when the big day comes

◯ your own small container of ibuprofen

◯ a few pieces of your all-time fave chocolate (to be replaced monthly!)

◯ a pair of clean underwear

◯ a plastic bag, like the kind produce comes in at the grocery store or a freezer bag that seals

◯ if you have a locker, an extra pair of jeans or uniform pants

◯ the backpack or bag you use for school, dance, sports

How to make it happen:

1. Tuck 3/4 of the pads or tampons into the Mini-Woman Kit you're keeping in your undies drawer, and put the other 1/4 of them into your backpack or

bag; some of those can be transferred to your locker if you have one.

2. Place the ibuprofen and the chocolate in the Mini-Woman Kit too, just in case you need them. Well, you *will* need the chocolate! (If you can't have chocolate, slip in another small treat you enjoy.)

3. Put the plastic bag, the extra undies, and the spare outfit bottoms in your backpack or bag. Transfer to your locker if you have one.

4. Pop the lid back on your kit, and take your travel pack/bag with you next time you head out for school or practice or any other place you'll be for more than an hour. For short shopping trips or going out to eat, one pad in your purse should do the trick. If you're not into purses, ask your mom to have one in hers.

You are ready for your first or next period, with no worries that it's going to be so embarrassing you'll have to move to a new town. With an easy mind, you can concentrate on the more fun parts of being a mini-woman.

That's What I'm Talkin' About

Having your period isn't just physical—it's emotional too. Here's your chance to sort some of that out . As always, you can either fill in your answers here or you can write/draw them in a special notebook.

Things to ponder when it's just you and God talkin':

If I had to describe my attitude about having periods, I would say, _____

_____.

The one person I really want to talk to about all this is ___

_____.

What's stopping me is _____

_____.

I'm still a little (or a lot or not at all) embarrassed about this whole thing because _____

_____.

I wish my family understood that_____

_____.

5

Confessions of a Couch Potato

When I bring up the subject of exercise with mini-women, I get everything from:

> I really hate to exercise because I'm kind of a girly-girl, so I don't like to mess up my hair, and I'm convinced that the worst thing on earth is to sweat.

To:

> I don't see how people can just sit down and stare at a computer screen all day. That is SOOOOO boring! I play soccer, I jog, I play field hockey, and I LOVE swimming. It all feels so good!

You probably already know that you *should* be moving around on a regular basis. Whether you *like* to or actually *do* it could be another matter, right? Even if you're a tween who can't possibly keep still—even in your sleep!—you might not know a whole lot about the "rights and wrongs" of exercise so you can have the healthiest body possible during these changing years.

So no matter what your exercise attitude, this chapter is for you. I promise it won't be a lecture to those of you who would rather curl up with a stack of good books all weekend or surf the Web instead of the waves. I also guarantee that you girl athletes won't find a list of do's and don'ts that'll empty out all the fun. My purpose here is to show all mini-women that exercise needs to be a part of your life, and that no matter who you are, it can be totally fun and safe and, as always, just right for you.

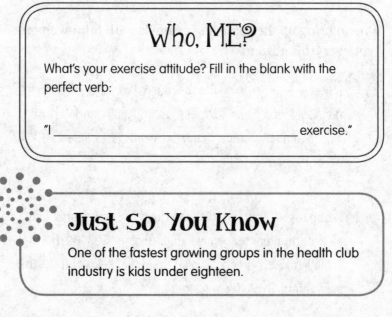

Who, ME?

What's your exercise attitude? Fill in the blank with the perfect verb:

"I _____ exercise."

Just So You Know

One of the fastest growing groups in the health club industry is kids under eighteen.

HERE'S THE DEAL ABOUT WHY YOU NEED TO EXERCISE

Okay, mini-women, let's get clear on one thing before we start talking about getting up and moving around. I'm going to encourage you to exercise so you'll be healthy and strong—*not* so you will lose weight and look like a starving model. Please, please (and did I mention please?) remember these three things:

1. Unless a *doctor* says you need to lose weight for your health, it is *not* good for you to go on a weight-loss program at this point in your life. Although exercise may trim you down some, that should not be your goal. Your goal is to be as healthy as you can be.

2. I said it in chapter 2, but let's say it again: Your body is growing fast right now in both height and weight. They probably won't both happen at the same time, so you may find yourself feeling chunky at some point until your height growth catches up to your weight growth. (Just as you might go through a period where your weight growth hasn't caught up to your height growth and you are sure you look like a stick of bamboo.) *Do not worry about it!* If you eat healthy and get good exercise, everything will balance out, and you will be the lovely young woman you were meant to be.

3. Very *few* girls look like models and actresses. In fact, some of *them* don't even look like their pictures. Most photos are "fixed" by computers to smooth out "flaws." Even if the girls *are* bone thin

with large breasts, they only make up a very small portion of the female population. The rest of us are gorgeous too, no matter what our shape. Get used to loving your body just the way it is on any given day. Love it so much you want to take care of it.

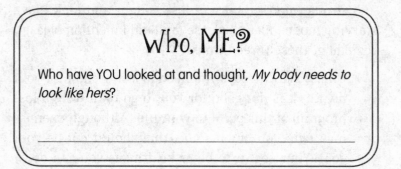

Who, ME?

Who have YOU looked at and thought, *My body needs to look like hers*?

_____

Just So You Know

Kids your age are now suffering from medical problems that used to happen only in adults—things like obesity (being extremely overweight), high blood pressure, high cholesterol, and Type II diabetes. All of that is connected with tweens not getting enough exercise.

GOT GOD?

As we're talking about exercise, it might help you to remember this way-important God-truth:

Your body isn't really "yours."

It actually belongs to God, and God has trusted you

with it. Your job is to take care of it so it'll be in the best shape possible ...

○ for the big-time important work God has given you to do.

○ so you can totally enjoy the gifts that are waiting for you.

Think of it this way: If God gave you his personal bicycle to use, wouldn't you make sure you kept it running right and looking good—and be extra careful not to smash it up? Who wants to go to God with something of his that's all messed up because you just sort of let it go? That's the way it works with your body.

The Bible gives you the perfect verse for this, and it's one you'll hear a lot as you get older:

> Do you not know that your bodies are temples of the Holy Spirit, who is in you, whom you have received from God? You are not your own; you were bought at a price. Therefore honor God with your bodies.
>
> 1 Corinthians 6:19–20

Exercise is one of the most important ways you can keep your "temple" in great condition. Thank God for your body, and then get it moving!

• •

❝I exercise because I want to be fit and flexible when I'm older. Not like my grandma.❞

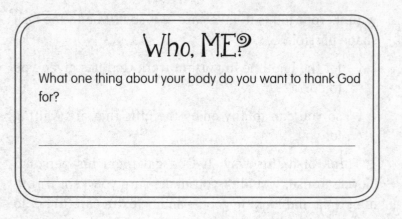

Who, ME?

What one thing about your body do you want to thank God for?

_____

_____

> Here's why I exercise: it's fun, you keep fit, you spend time with friends, and you make new ones.

HERE'S THE DEAL ABOUT WHAT EXERCISE DOES FOR YOU

Let's look at this in mini-woman terms. Exercise:

- *gives you energy and staying power* so you can do all the cool things you want to do; that includes the stamina for writing great poetry as much as it does the juice for scoring soccer goals.

- *helps you sleep*; no more tossing and turning and freaking out because you're wide awake after lights out.

- *makes your muscles stronger and more flexible,* which not only feels great, but also *looks* great on you. Who doesn't want that?

- *makes your eyes sparkle and your skin glow*; yeah, even when you're PMS-y.

- *builds your confidence* so you don't break out in hives every time you have to give a presentation in class or try to make new friends.

- *makes your mind sharper*; a better grasp of fractions and commas, anyone?

- *keeps you from getting all bummed out*; girls who stay reasonably active have fewer of those mood swings we've been talking about; it's hard to stay all funky when you're out having a good time.

" I hate admitting it, but I'm really kind of lazy. **"**

Who, ME?

Put an exclamation point (!) next to all the items on that list above that YOU want.

"So, how *much* exercise do I need?" (asks the girl who loves her down time!) Let's find out where you are now and that will help you figure out not only how *much*, but also what *kind* of regular movement is right for the unique you.

"It just seems like there are more things to do inside the house. What can't you do on the computer?"

That Is SO Me!

Read each sentence starter below, and circle the answer that comes closest to describing you. There's no right and wrong here—there's just you!

1. I would rather

   a. play on a sports team.

   b. do gymnastics or cheers or dance moves with my friends.

   c. read a book on a porch swing.

2. If I could have a new top-of-the-line item, it would be

   a. soccer cleats, a basketball hoop, a softball glove.

   b. a bike, skates, or snorkeling gear.

   c. an iPad, a cell phone, or a digital camera.

3. If my friend's family invited me to go on a daylong hike with them, I would

   a. be totally jazzed.

   b. say yes, but wonder if I could actually walk for a whole day.

   c. say no and wish they'd invited me to a movie marathon instead.

4. If we had to run a track in PE, I

   a. wouldn't be able to talk because I'd be running so hard.

b. would be able to talk but not sing because I'd be running.

c. could probably sing a whole musical because I'd be strolling.

5. When I'm exercising my favorite way, I think about

a. winning or beating my own personal best.

b. what a blast I'm having.

c. um—I don't have a favorite exercise.

Let's see what your answers say about you—and remember that the purpose here is to show you how to use this chapter in a way that's right for YOU.

If you had mostly a's, girl, you are a serious athlete and you *love* competition. You probably get plenty of exercise, which is great. Just be sure to let an adult know if you ever experience any of these things while you're playing or practicing: pain, nausea, dizziness, or sudden major tiredness. It could mean you're working your body too hard. Otherwise, as long as exercise is fun for you, keep doing what you're doing! And keep reading. There's still important info in this chapter for you.

If you had mostly b's, exercise is a total joy when it's something you can do on your own or during free time with your friends or family. Great fitness plan! Be sure you get some of that physical activity every day, and keep on enjoying it the way you do. This chapter will help you get the *most* out of your fun.

If you had mostly c's, you don't get your body moving on a regular basis, right? Whether it's because you think you're a klutz when you try to play sports, or you feel too sluggish and tired to be active, or somebody has made fun of you for the way you move, exercise probably isn't your favorite thing. That's not your fault, and you know what? You don't have to be a soccer star or even feel all that graceful on a pair of skates to enjoy some kind of activity. Let's see if we can find something fun for you in this chapter—something that will get your heart rate up and increase your breathing to get you healthier. You only have to do it for twenty minutes a day, three times a week, but if you discover your personal exercise thing, you'll feel so good you'll want to do it more.

> I'm a total dancer nerd! I dance twenty-two hours a week. Injuries? OH, yeah: pulled muscles, twisted ankles/knees, sprains, random bruises, various unexplainable pains ...

Just So You Know

Exercise ISN'T the best thing if you get hurt. Always:

- Follow the safety rules in any physical activity.
- Start slow and give your body time to warm up.

If you're biking, in-line skating, or skateboarding, wear a helmet and knee pads. If you're playing basketball, wear high-tops. If you're practicing a sport on your own, wear the same protective gear as when you're with your coach.

If you get hurt today, you won't be out there having fun tomorrow.

66 I was playing dodgeball with some kids who were really rough, and I broke the growth plate on my finger. Now it doesn't grow! 99

66 The truth is, I just don't have TIME to be healthy! 99

Just So You Know

Aerobic exercise is brisk exercise that gets oxygen moving through your blood and increases how fast you breathe. Think running, swimming, and bicycling.

Just So You Know

Only 25 percent of eighth graders are required to take physical education in school. That means you're pretty much on your own when it comes to getting enough exercise!

Who, ME?

The last time I got twenty minutes of aerobic exercise was

_____.

Other mini-women's whose fave ways to exercise are:

- Running around with friends.
- Playing softball, volleyball, basketball, soccer, field hockey, badminton, tennis, dodge ball.
- Riding bikes.
- Swimming.
- Dancing.
- Doing gymnastics.
- Horseback riding.
- In-line skating.

HERE'S THE DEAL FOR A PERSONAL FITNESS PLAN

The only really good exercise is exercise that you enjoy and will keep doing without having to bribe yourself. Even if your schedule is already packed with sports and lessons, check out these steps. You may find a small change you want to make so your exercise program can rock even more.

Step One—*Decide that you're going to do some kind of aerobic exercise at least twenty minutes a day, three days a week.* That's the very minimum. The more you do, the better for your body—as long as you don't feel sick or injure yourself. If you aren't sure you can make that promise to yourself, tell a grown-up what you want to do and ask that person to help you stay with it. Putting it on a sign and posting it where you can see it will really help.

Step Two—*Choose an activity* (or several, so you don't get bored doing the same thing all the time).

1. Choose an activity that is *aerobic* (increases your heart rate and makes you breathe harder than usual). Twenty minutes' worth is best, and a good rule of thumb is that while you're exercising, you should be able to talk fairly easily but not sing a song. Riding a bike, walking a dog, and dancing to fast music can all be aerobic. Doing one cartwheel, playing a video game, and walking from the TV to the refrigerator are not!

2. *Choose something that fits your personality.* If you like to compete and you think games with teams and rules are fun, definitely play a sport. If you're a free spirit, pick an individual activity like bike riding, skating, or swimming. If you're the happiest when you're hanging out with your friends, select something you can all do together that doesn't have a lot of rules and structure. That could be anything from shooting baskets in your driveway to organizing a skating party in your cul-de-sac. If you're a curl-up-with-a-book girl, find something practical that doesn't even seem like exercise. Can you walk to the library? Play backyard games with your little brothers and sisters to give your mom a break? Make up your own story in your head while you jog?

3. *Make sure it fits into your family's lifestyle and schedule.* You might decide you want to ice-skate three times a week, but if the rink is on the other side of town and your mom is already spending ten hours

a week chauffeuring everybody around … you get the idea.

Step Three—*Set a goal for yourself.* Make it something you can eventually do but is hard enough so you can say, "Hey, I did that!" when you reach it. Be sure you'll be able to tell if you get there. "I want to be able to skate longer" won't be as helpful as "I want to be able to skate for thirty minutes without having to sit down because I'm tired." Here are some examples of good fitness goals:

- Swim the whole length of the pool three times without stopping.

- Stay in the whole soccer game without getting too tired to play.

- Ride my bike to school for ten school days in a row instead of asking my mom to give me a ride.

- Play two straight hours of nonstop hopscotch for the neighborhood record.

If you don't have trouble getting yourself to exercise, let your goal be something wild, like doing twenty cartwheels in a clown suit. Just a thought.

Step Four—*Set up a fitness schedule for yourself* if you don't already have one (like practicing with your team several times a week, for example). Look for details about setting up a schedule in "You Can Do It" at the end of this chapter.

Step Five—*Decide how you'll reward yourself when you've reached your goal.* Will you use your saved-up allowance to download a new album to dance to? Read your favorite book all the way through again? Make yourself a killer smoothie? God smiles on you when you make an effort to take care of that body, so make plans to smile on *yourself* with a treat.

Step Six—*Once you've reached your goal and rewarded yourself, set a new goal and a new reward.* After all, you're never finished exercising. You're starting a lifelong habit.

Just So You Know

Some of the most fun exercise involves your whole family. If your dad suggests a group bike ride or hike, give it a try even if it sounds worse than having a cavity filled. If you can think of activities you, your siblings, and your parents could get into together, speak up. (Your brothers will only complain until they start having a blast.)

Who, ME?

What is your fave way to get exercise (even if you seldom get to do it)?

_____

_____

_____

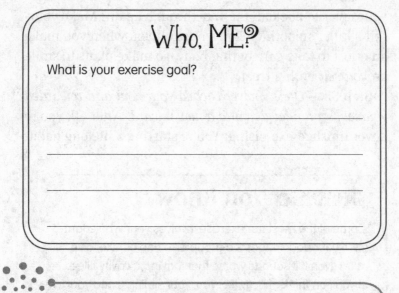

Who, ME?

What is your exercise goal?

_____

_____

_____

_____

Just So You Know

Smaller goals you can reach quickly so you can move on to the next goal are better than huge ones it could take years to accomplish.

GOOD: Swim three laps without stopping.

NOT AS GOOD: Make the US Olympic swimming team.

Just So You Know

It usually takes two weeks for something new in a person's life to become a habit.

Who, ME?

What would your perfect goal-reaching reward be?

_____

_____

Just So You Know

There's nothing wrong with playing video games, looking things up on the computer, watching TV or movies, and reading. But if you're spending more than two hours a day doing any of them, you're cutting into moving-around time. Since you already sit a lot in school and when you're doing homework, riding in the car, and eating, if you spend too much more time on your buns, you won't burn enough calories to keep your body in good condition. Do your reading and computer time after you walk the dog or have that wild game of hide-and-seek with your buds.

66 I usually stretch while I study. 99

66 When I get restless, I just ride my bike around the yard. 99

> **I** like exercise I can do without thinking about it being exercise. You know, like swimming or walking to get ice cream with my friends. **"**

> **My** life is too crazy busy for my exercise, but my mom and I go for walks. I don't know if that counts, but it's really special. **"**

> **I'm** always the slowest one in sports. I'd rather be writing! **"**

HERE'S THE DEAL ABOUT SLEEP

Just as important as exercise is its opposite—rest. Whether you snooze like a kitten or would love to stay up all night, these guidelines are for you:

1. *Get enough sleep* so that when you get up in the morning, you're wide awake and alert within fifteen to thirty minutes (even if you aren't a "morning person").

2. *Be sure "enough sleep" is at LEAST eight hours a night.*

3. *Try to go to bed and get up at the same times,* except on weekends and holidays. (Even then, don't get off your routine more than an hour or two.)

4. *Sleep in loose, soft clothing.* Be sure you won't be too hot or too cold.

> I can NEVER get to sleep! I have to turn off my light at ten, but usually my head is so full of different ideas for books and stuff I'm reading and all my problems, that I can't fall asleep until at least eleven. And some nights I have dreams that don't conclude, so I wake up at three in the morning and imagine an ending.

5. *Have a regular, unwinding routine that you follow before bed so you can fall asleep within a half hour.* Maybe it's a hot bath, a protein snack like turkey, and nighttime prayers. Some girls like to write in a journal to sort out all the stuff of the day. Others let music calm them down. Going to sleep with the TV on isn't the best choice.

6. *You'll sleep best if your room doesn't look like an earthquake hit it.* Tidy up some before you crawl under the covers.

> I don't get enough sleep. I can't FALL asleep, so I go on my iPod or read a book and the next time I look at the clock, it's really late. Then I have to get up early. It's not pretty.

Who, ME?

The number of hours YOU sleep on a school night: _____

7. *Within two hours before bedtime, don't drink caffeine, eat a big meal, or watch scary or upsetting TV or movies.* Don't exercise right before you climb into bed either.

8. *If you lie awake for longer than a half hour every night or have major nightmares, talk to your mom or dad about it.* You may have things bothering you that even you don't know about.

Who, ME?

My favorite pj's?

_____

Who, ME?

What YOU do thirty minutes before you turn out your light.

_____

_____

66 I'm not a good sleeper and it takes me FOREVER to fall asleep. My dad and I go for little walks before bed and that helps. 99

> **When I'm super excited about something, that's when it takes me, like, thirty minutes to get to sleep!**

Who, ME?

What keeps YOU awake?

_____

_____

_____

YOU CAN DO IT

Creating a Sisterhood, Part 4

Ready to get the sisterhood together again?

1. Decide ahead of time *what kind* of moving around you'd like to do together. Be sure it's something everybody will enjoy—anything from a just-for-fun series of soccer drills to a dance marathon with your mom's Oldies collection. As long as you can do it nonstop for twenty minutes, you're good to go.

2. That will determine *where* you need to meet. If everyone is up for a wacky obstacle course, you'll want to gather outside. If you're going to teach each other new dance moves, inside might be better.

3. When you're all ready (and the safety rules are in place—like helmets if you're going for a bike ride or an adult present if you're swimming in a pool)—set a timer for twenty minutes and go for it. The goal is to have a moving-around blast that will get everyone's heart rate and breathing into higher gear. If you're having too much fun to stop at twenty, keep going until you're all a sweaty mess!

4. Be sure to have water on hand for everyone. While you're sipping, see if you can figure out these things as a group:

   • Is this something you want to do together on a regular basis? How could you make it even more fun?

   • How can you help each other keep up your individual exercise? Make a chart with stickers? Pass each other Girl-Grams when you reach goals? Plan a celebration when everybody meets the same goal?

   • What's hard about keeping up with exercise? What ideas do you have for fixing that? For instance, if you all love to ride bikes but finding a safe place to do it is tough, could you research nearby bike trails and ask the moms and dads to rotate going along to supervise?

5. If you're up for it and time allows, you can make personal fitness logs together. (See Mini-Woman Kit below.)

6. Make a promise to pray for each other. And, hey, why not circle up and pray together before you dash off to the next healthy, heart-racing thing?

Your Mini-Woman Kit, Part 4

What you're doing:

Serious athletes keep a log of their activities—often in a small book. You can put one together, especially designed for the unique YOU, and keep it in your Mini-Woman Kit.

What you'll need:

○ the fitness plan information and choices you gathered in steps one through six under "Here's the Deal ..." on pages 110-113.

○ a blank book or paper in a small binder, purchased or homemade (with heavier paper or cardboard for the cover and blank white pages stapled inside)

○ a cool pen or marker

○ pictures of your favorite sports or activities from magazines or your own photo collection

○ glue stick or tape

How to make it happen:

1. Decorate your blank book however you want with pictures and quotes to inspire you.

2. Set up a page for each week.

   • Put your goal at the top, and divide the page into three columns.

   • Down the left side, list the days and times you're going to work toward your goal.

- In the center column, write what you actually do, for how long, how many times, and those kinds of things.

- On the right, you can make notes, such as, "This is getting easier," "Coach said I was improving," and "I think my tennis shoes are too small."

3. You can design one section of the book for listing ways you'd like to reward yourself so when you meet your goal, you can choose one. That's a fun section for "dream pictures."

4. Tuck your book into your Mini-Woman Kit so you'll know right where it is as you do your check-ins.

5. When you reach your goal, set up a new one—with new rewards! When you can actually see yourself making progress, you'll want to make even more.

That's What I'm Talkin' About

You're only going to keep exercising if YOU really want to. Thinking these things through and discussing them with God will help you get there. As always, you can either just fill in your answers here or you can write/draw them in a special notebook.

If I could do any kind of exercise/sport/physical activity I wanted (and the time and money were there for me to do it), I would _____

_____

_____.

I would exercise more if _____

_____

_____.

One person who could help me get moving is _____

_____

_____.

I think my body is worth taking care of because _____

_____

_____.

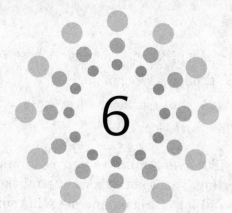

6

Table Talk

It's not hard to get tween girls talking about food—ya think?—and what you mini-women have to say about it is pretty interesting.

66 If I ate the way I WANTED every dayÐcandy and ice cream and milkshakesÐI would weigh 300 pounds! 99

66 I have weird food allergies, so I always consider choosing food to be a game. Who says you shouldn't play with your food? 99

> I love eating in the summertime best, with all the fresh produce around in this farm country. We don't go a day without farm-fresh produce. My mouth is watering ...

Sounds like every mini-woman is unique when it comes to eating. That's not a shock by now, right? Yet just as with everything else about this stage in your life, some basics apply to *all* tween girls. Before we talk about what those are (and I promise they won't include "You have to eat brussels sprouts!"), let's see what *you're* putting into your body these days.

> I love stromboli.

> Mmmmm ... homemade cheese ravioli.

Who, ME?

What's the first thing that comes to mind when YOU hear the word *food*?

_____

_____

> I dig organic pop tarts for breakfast.

> Sometimes I just like to have an apple.

That Is SO Me!

This quiz isn't here to make you feel guilty about the things you're chowing down on. Think of it instead as an eye-opener. You can only get healthy if you see where you're food challenged.

Under each menu, circle the number that's closest to what you eat most often for that meal. (Not the one you think you *should* eat, but the one that actually goes into your mouth!)

Breakfast Menu

1. donut, muffin, or microwave/toaster treat

2. cold cereal, toast, or waffles/pancakes

3. fruit, yogurt, or a smoothie

4. eggs, a smoothie with protein powder, or hot cereal

Morning Snack Menu

1. donut, muffin, or candy bar

2. granola bar, crackers and cheese, or fruit juice

3. fresh fruit, yogurt, or dried fruit (like raisins)

4. celery with peanut butter, trail mix, or a glass of milk

Lunch Menu

1. pizza, chicken nuggets, or a burger and fries

2. lunch meat, cheese, or PB&J on white or wheat bread

3. tuna, chicken, or turkey sandwich on whole-grain bread

4. veggie soup, tuna, or chicken on salad or turkey wrap with lettuce and tomatoes

Afternoon Snack Menu

1. cookies, chips, or a microwaved snack like Hot Pockets

2. popcorn, pretzels, or a milk shake

3. peanut butter and whole-wheat crackers, a fruit smoothie, or a bowl of non-sugary cereal

4. raw veggies, fresh fruit, or no-sugar-added yogurt

Dinner Menu

1. frozen dinner, pizza, or supper at a fast-food restaurant

2. fried chicken and mashed potatoes, SpaghettiOs and applesauce, or macaroni and cheese

3. steak, baked potato, and salad; or barbecue chicken, rice, and peas

4. baked chicken, broccoli, and green salad; or broiled fish, string beans, and fruit salad

Bedtime Snack Menu

1. cookies and milk, cereal with sugar and milk, or a pudding cup

2. popcorn, fruit juice, or chocolate milk

3. peanut butter and crackers, cheese, or plain milk

4. turkey slice, decaffeinated tea with milk, or warm milk

Were you totally, 100 percent honest? Okay, then add together the numbers you've circled. You'll come up with a total between 6 and 24, which you can write here: _____

Let's see what that might say about your "fuel supply."

If your total was between 6 and 9, your diet has some pretty big nutrition holes in it. You're probably not getting very many of the things you need to be strong and healthy and to grow as much as you need to. You may even get sick a lot. That can be fixed, and this chapter will show you how. For now, do *not* go to your mom and tell her she's not feeding you right!

If your total is between 10 and 14, you're getting some of the things from food that you need for health and growth, but you'd feel better and have more energy if you ate more nutritious foods. That can be fixed too. Meanwhile, don't complain about your diet to your mom! This chapter is about *your* choices.

If your total is between 15 and 19, you have a pretty healthy diet, and it probably shows in how you feel and how much energy you have. Even if you didn't change a thing, you'd be healthy and strong. This chapter will just help you see any gaps you might have in your diet that could be filled with some even yummier things.

If your total is between 20 and 24, you're very unusual for your age! You have an excellent chance of being in amazing physical shape. It's okay, by the way, to treat yourself to a little fun "kid food" once in a while. Read on for some safe ways to do that.

HERE'S THE DEAL ABOUT WHAT YOU NEED TO EAT

Between all the growing you're doing and the exercise you're getting—you *are*, aren't you?—you obviously need the right fuel, and not just anything you can get your hands on, but the real stuff your body needs for all the moving and changing it's doing.

This is the **Pyramid Plan** designed by the USDA, the US Department of Agriculture (the people who study this stuff for a living). It shows how much you should eat from each food group compared to the other groups. The columns are wider on the bottom to remind you to eat more of the leaner choices from each category.

make half your grains whole

get your calcium-rich foods

vary your veggies

focus on fruits

know your fats

go lean on protein

These **Pyramid Guidelines** will help you use that pyramid.

Grains

> Make at least half your grains whole grains.
>> 1 slice of bread
>> 1 cup dry cereal
>> ½ cup cooked rice, pasta, or cereal

Vegetables

> Color your plate with all kinds of great-tasting veggies.
>> 2½ cups Dark green, orange, dry beans and peas, or other pretty veggies

Fruits
    Make most choices fruit, not juice.
        1½ cups
Milk
    Choose fat-free or low-fat dairy most often.
        1 cup yogurt
        1½ ounces cheese
        1 cup milk
Meat and Beans
    Choose lean meat and chicken or turkey.
    Vary your choices—more fish, beans, peas, nuts, and seeds.
        1 egg
        1 tablespoon peanut butter
        ½ ounce nuts
        or ¼ cup dry beans (cooked, of course!)

Those quantities are designed for a girl of ten who does thirty to sixty minutes of physical activity a day (the steps on the pyramid are a reminder of the importance of exercise). If you want to have a more unique-to-you plan, go to *www.MyPyramid.gov* and the website will show you how.

" My family and me call me a grainatarian! "

" When you have healthy options, you usually make them ... with a treat now and then! "

┌───┐

Who, ME?

Draw a spoon next to each USDA guideline that will be
hard for YOU to follow.

└───┘

HERE'S THE DEAL ABOUT WHAT YOU SHOULDN'T EAT A LOT OF

You may be thinking, "Uh, where do my sodas and candy bars and salad dressing and stuff go on the pyramid?" They actually don't fit into any group. They're extras that are mainly fat and sugar, and you should use them *sparingly*. **Sparingly** means:

- *No more than 60 grams of fat a day.* A Double Whopper with cheese and mayo has 69 grams of fat. If you become a label reader, you'll discover how fast those fats can add up.

- *No more than 10 teaspoons of sugar a day.* That may sound like a lot, but it adds up fast. With your mom's permission, measure 18 teaspoons of sugar into a glass of water. Would you drink that? Yuck! But that's how much sugar is in a 20-ounce bottle of soda. A Cinnabon has 11 teaspoons of sugar. A 12-ounce McFlurry with M&Ms has 18 teaspoons of sugar. Check the labels of things like salad dressing, spaghetti sauce, and soup, and try not to eat anything with more than 4 grams of sugar (5 grams equals about one teaspoon).

Who, ME?

Read the label on YOUR fave snack food. How much fat and sugar does it have? Does that make you go, "Oh, good!" or "Uh-oh!"?

_____

Just So You Know

While you're chowing down on good food, remember to drink water. Your body is ninety percent water, so you need lots—like six glasses a day. Soda, juice, and milk don't count—it has to be plain old H_2O. A lot of girls say they don't like water, but that's probably because they're used to trying to quench their thirst with other things that, quite frankly, taste better. But once you develop the water habit, you'll learn to love it, really. Nothing takes away thirst better, and it gives you so much energy. In fact, next time you're really hungry and it isn't mealtime, drink a big glass of water and see if that helps. Sometimes when you think you're hungry, your body is really telling you it's thirsty.

HERE'S THE DEAL ABOUT WHAT TO NEVER EAT!

Your pencil eraser.

No, seriously, there are some foods that just don't help your body and can actually hurt it. Once in a while, okay, but you can enjoy substitutes that actually *do* something for you. BTW, foods that give you absolutely nothing are called **empty calories**.

On the left you'll find the **empty calories**. On the right are things you can enjoy instead.

Unhealthy Choices:	Healthy Alternatives:
soda	milk
	fruit juice (½ cup a day)
	water with lemon or lime
artificial sweeteners	1 tsp. of honey
	a dash of brown sugar
	cinnamon
any foods with sugar as the first ingredient listed on a package	fruit
	raisins
	fruit spread on bread
crackers and chips that contain partially hydrogenated oil	pretzels
	whole-grain crackers
	high-fiber graham crackers
	rice cakes with natural peanut butter
margarine	Smart Balance
	a little real butter
snacks and cereals made with corn	cereals made with whole grain or rice (the first ingredient should be "whole grain")
store-bought cookies	homemade cookies baked with whole-wheat flour, brown sugar, and other healthy ingredients

> I wonder if fruit and stuff was unhealthy, would we like it more, and if candy was healthy, we wouldn't like it so much?

Who, ME?

A food YOU probably need to cut down on is:

_____

Just So You Know

Sometimes the crankiness of puberty is about low blood sugar, and that's easy to fix with a small nutritious snack. Mini-women tell me they get crabby either at midmorning or right as school lets out. Their fave mood lifters are:

- raspberry yogurt
- graham crackers
- peanut butter and Nutella on bread
- pretzels
- granola bar
- a handful of almonds
- dried fruit
- veggies with hummus
- smoothie

All GREAT choices! Go mini-women!

HERE'S THE DEAL ON WHAT TO EAT WHEN

Certain foods will fuel you better if you eat them at the right times. Try these "timed treats," and you will *rock*!

For all-day energy

- Start off with a healthy breakfast, even if it isn't breakfast food. Who says you can't have a turkey sandwich first thing in the morning?

- Eat a healthy snack at midmorning and in the midafternoon. Three meals are not enough to get you through the day. You need body and brain food every few hours. Ya gotta love that, right?

For a big-test day (especially those standardized tests that come every couple of years and last all day)

- Eat an especially good breakfast.

- Avoid sugary snacks that will make you sleepy once the big energy spike is gone.

Before really strenuous physical activity (like a game, a big practice or a family hike)

- Eat complex carbohydrates like fruit, whole-grain bread, or raw veggies, which will burn while you're active and keep giving you energy.

- Eating a sweet snack will give you a burst, but it won't last long, and when it's gone, you'll *crash*!

To help you fall asleep quickly and easily at night

- Do *not* eat foods containing sugar or anything really fatty or greasy within two hours of going to bed.

- Do *not* drink any caffeine within six hours of going to bed. That means no cola after midafternoon (or ever if you can manage that).

- *Do* eat turkey before you go to bed if you have trouble falling asleep. It has tryptophan in it, which promotes sleepiness if you eat it on an empty tummy.

- Milk is good before bed too, especially if it's warmed up with cinnamon. Yum.

- The later dinner is, the lighter it should be. If you're having supper after seven o'clock, eat veggies, whole grains, and lean protein like turkey or chicken, rather than a big ol' steak with a baked potato and sour cream or a huge plate of spaghetti.

Who, ME?

What's in YOUR house that you could eat before bed?

_____

_____

Just So You Know

The sugar we eat is usually refined sugar, which does this in our bodies:

> Step 1: Ups our blood sugar level (makes sense, right?)

> Step 2: Gives us instant energy (that "sugar high" you hear about)

> Step 3: Causes higher insulin levels that can leave you feeling shaky

> Step 4: Once that's gone, our energy drops big time (some people call that a "crash"), so what was the point of eating it in the first place?

White flour isn't wonderful for us either. It doesn't have any fiber (or "roughage") to help our bodies eliminate what they don't use (in other words, "poop"). Basically we need to keep fruits, veggies, and grains as close to their natural state as we can.

And if food contains high fructose corn syrup, run away!

HERE'S THE DEAL ABOUT FAST FOOD

It's so fun to go to McDonald's with the team after a big victory, or have breakfast at Burger King with your dad on Saturday morning before you hit the mall together. Go! Enjoy! Just don't do it every day or even every week if you can help it. Here's why:

- The food is super processed, which means it's loaded with chemicals that are hard on your liver, your heart, and your stomach.

- It's high in fat, which is hard to digest and adds calories that stay on you instead of burning off; the fried stuff is the worst.

- The bread (usually) isn't whole grain, so it has more sugar and doesn't have the fiber you need for your digestion.

- The portions are way too big; one Double Whopper with cheese and mayo has 1,060 calories—and you only need a total of 1,800 in a whole day!

- Some "meals" automatically come with a soda, which is loaded with salt and sugar; its carbonation has acid, which isn't good for your tummy, teeth, or bones.

" Sometimes I crave a brownie a la mode from Chik-fil-A. "

When you do go out for fast food on a fun occasion, the following menu items are your best choices because they have the least amount of calories, salt, chemicals, and unhealthy fat:

- KFC—Original Recipe Chicken Breast without skin or breading
- Burger King—Chicken Whopper (without mayo) or BK Veggie Burger
- McDonald's—Plain Hamburger
- Subway—Veggie Delite 6-inch sub
- Taco Bell—Fresco-Style Crunchy Taco
- Wendy's—Jr. Hamburger

Forget the fries (most of the time), and go for the fruit some fast-food places now offer. Choose milk or orange juice or water to drink.

HERE'S THE DEAL ABOUT CHOICES

You might be really jazzed about eating a healthier diet, but you may also be thinking, "Hello-o! I don't do the grocery shopping. I don't decide what we have for dinner."

Well, there is that, isn't there?

Plus, many families are so busy with sports practices and after-school lessons and church activities, dinner's often served from a drive-through window and eaten in the backseat of the car. Even if you do eat at home, meals might be popped out of a box because there's so much going on.

> Everyone who's there eats together at the table, and we wait for the blessing to be said.

> We aren't allowed to have cell phones at the table.

But did you know that young people your age influence (on average) one out of every three spending decisions a family makes? Usually that means kids are whining for X-Boxes, iPads, and cell phones—but why not put in your vote for healthier food? (And, again, do *not* tell your parents they've been feeding you all wrong and you are now going to set them straight; they won't appreciate it!) Here are some ways you can take charge of your food choices:

- **Volunteer to go grocery shopping with whomever does that chore in your family**. And instead of begging for the cereal with the marshmallows, ask for a whole-grain choice that doesn't have more than 4 grams of sugar per serving. See if your mom or dad will buy grapes instead of cookies, whole-wheat bread instead of white, and pretzels instead of chips. They may want to know who you are and what you've done with their daughter, but when they recover, they'll probably be proud of you.

- **Ask if you can help plan meals for the week**. Make a cool menu sheet by hand or on the computer to post on the refrigerator. Ask family members what they want for suppers, and use this book to make their selections as healthy as possible.

- **Hang out in the kitchen, and help with the cooking.** If your parents don't have time to chop up stuff for a salad, you can totally do that. If it's too hectic in the afternoon for Mom to make smoothies before soccer practice, step up to the plate (or blender) yourself and do it.

MENU	Breakfast	Lunch	Dinner
Sunday			
Monday			
Tuesday			
Wednesday			
Thursday			
Friday			
Saturday			

66 Most of the time I make something (leftovers or a sandwich) and eat by myself on the couch or on my bed. My parents split about a year ago, and the last time I remember eating dinner as a family was when I was six. 99

66 We sit on stools at the counter and have somewhat healthy things. 99

> **We** sit around the coffee table and eat and talk and watch TV.

- *Pack your own nutritious lunch, since school lunch isn't always the healthiest meal on the planet.* Include baby carrots and grapes instead of chips and cookies. Make a killer sandwich that will have everybody at the table drooling. Pop in the occasional treat—like homemade cookies—maybe on Fridays.

- *When Mom and Dad want to know where you'd like to eat out,* don't automatically shout for your favorite pizza place, or if you do, get a salad and eat it before you dig into a double cheese with pepperoni.

- *When you're hanging out with your friends, grab a juice or water instead of a soda.* Eat one handful of chips instead of half the bag. Better yet, carry raisins, healthy crackers, or a small bag of trail mix in your backpack.

If anybody teases you about your healthy eating habits, that's one of the few times it's appropriate to roll your eyes. (Unless it's at your mom or dad; you have to put up with them!) Why let some unhealthy person tell you how to eat? You have the power to feed yourself the right way, so smile and chomp away on that celery stick with natural peanut butter. Then knock their socks off on the soccer field, in the spelling bee, or at the next sleepover laugh fest, because you can do that when you fuel your body with the best stuff possible.

Who, ME?

Draw a fork next to each of those things on the previous two pages you can do for YOUR family.

HERE'S THE DEAL ON HELPING YOUR WHOLE FAMILY CHANGE THEIR EATING HABITS

As I've said (several times!), it isn't a good idea to announce to your parents that the way they're feeding you is appalling and you want it changed. There *are* kinder ways to handle it, ways that might even get results. Here are a few suggestions:

- Always ask if you can make a suggestion, rather than barging right in and saying, "Okay, I'm going to show you people how this is done."

- Explain that you know how hard it is to feed a family a healthy diet and that you just want to help by sharing what you're learning.

- Volunteer to help, rather than saying, "Mom, *you* should feed us way differently than you're doing now."

- Be sure you can commit on a regular basis to whatever you volunteer to do. Going to the store and talking Mom into buying fresh veggies and then disappearing when it's time to wash and chop them isn't going to win you any friends in the kitchen.

"Everyone who's there eats together at the table, and we wait for the blessing to be said."

"We aren't allowed to have cell phones at the table."

GOT GOD?

It doesn't take a rocket scientist to figure out that God is behind this whole feed-your-body-right thing. There are hundreds of verses about food in the Bible. Here are just a few of the things God says about how we should eat.

God said, "I give you every seed-bearing plant on the face of the whole earth and every tree that has fruit with seed in it. They will be yours for food."

Genesis 1:29

Sure sounds like fruits and veggies and grains. You don't hear anything about Twinkies and Pop-Tarts in there, do you?

Of all the animals that live on land, these are the ones you may eat.

Leviticus 11:2

God goes on to give forty-six verses worth of instructions about what animals to eat and how to cook them. Does it sound to you like God cares about the meat we put into our bodies? The point is not that we follow all of that exactly—although how hard would it be not to eat camel, rabbit, or vulture meat?—but that we pay attention to how natural and well-cooked our meat is. It's safe to say God did not envision a flat burger that's made mostly of icky fillers that clog up your body.

When you sit to dine with a ruler,
note well what is before you,
and put a knife to your throat
if you are given to gluttony.
Do not crave his delicacies,
for that food is deceptive.

Proverbs 23:1–3

Before you freak out, this doesn't mean you should literally take a blade to your neck! Those verses tell you several things:

- Don't think stuffing yourself with sweet, gooey,

creamy treats is going to make you happy or accepted.

- If you catch yourself eating junk when you're nervous or upset or unhappy, stop! Cut off that habit (not your throat), and do something healthy for yourself: talk to someone about what's bothering you, get some exercise to clear your head, or write to God in a journal about your troubles.

- If overeating and weighing so much that you can't enjoy physical activities or fun clothes are part of your life, ask a grown-up to help you. It isn't about being skinny; it's about how you feel in mind and body.

> When you have eaten and are satisfied, praise the Lord your God for the good land he has given you.
>
> Deuteronomy 8:10

God is warning us here not to take all the credit for the good things that happen to us. But this verse is also a reminder to be grateful for all the wonderful food choices we have and to eat and be satisfied.

That means:

- Don't let yourself get way too hungry because you think you'll get fat if you eat.

- Don't skip breakfast or lunch because you want to be skinny like the models in the magazines.

- Don't go on a weight-loss diet unless a *doctor* says you need to for health reasons—and even then, eat healthy food and get exercise instead of starving yourself.

You are not too young to be in danger of developing an **eating disorder**, such as **anorexia**, where a person deprives herself of food to the point of illness, or **bulimia**, where she stuffs in as much food as she can and then throws it up. If you are tempted to do either of these, go to an adult you trust immediately. An eating disorder is a sickness that can follow you your whole life if it isn't treated right away. You are a growing young woman. Eat, and be satisfied!

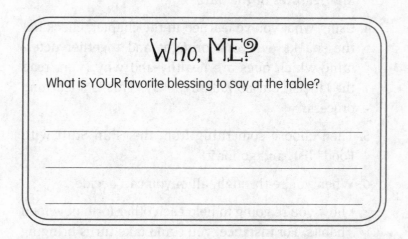

Who, ME?

What is YOUR favorite blessing to say at the table?

_____

_____

_____

YOU CAN DO IT

You may be ready to go all out on this healthy eating thing, or you may only have a little bit of time and need to start small. Just choose as many suggestions as you want from the "Fun Stuff with Food" list below that sound cool to you. Make a list for your Mini-Woman Kit and for your sisterhood for a group activity. Whatever you do, do it in joy!

Creating a Sisterhood, Part 5

1. When you're ready to get together again, ask everybody to bring what she considers a healthy snack.

2. The kitchen or breakfast nook or dining room is the perfect place for this little gathering. I mean, it makes sense, right?

3. Do as a group whatever you found fun in this chapter, just to get things going. Maybe some of the Who, ME? features or the quiz.

4. Using what you've learned in the chapter, check out the snacks everyone brought and together determine which ones are healthy and why (yup, read the labels). But no judging, okay? This is a learning process.

5. Then choose something from the "Fun Stuff with Food" list, and go for it!

6. When you're through, all of you can decide

   • how you're going to help each other form new food habits. For instance, you could take turns bringing the nutritious midmorning snack to school.

   • how you'll support each other in not getting hung up on being thin or feeling all guilty about the occasional treat. For example, make a vow to refuse to answer the question "Do I look fat to you?"

   • how you'll pray for each other (and do it now).

Your Mini-Woman Kit, Part 5

Choose any of the following suggestions that sound way fun to do on your own. Suggestions 1 and 3 include items you can put in your kit.

Fun stuff with food:

Suggestion 1: Make a very cool worksheet to write down what food you could eat for the next four days (within your control, of course). The food pyramid and guidelines can help you. It might look like this, with your own creative touches added, naturally. Check off the things you actually eat (and pencil in things you ate that you hadn't planned to eat). At the end of the four days, see how you're doing. This can be tucked into your Mini-Woman Kit.

Meals	Day One	Day Two	Day Three	Day Four
Breakfast				
Midmorning Snack				
Lunch				
Midafternoon Snack				
Dinner				
Bedtime Snack				

Suggestion 2: Plan the most nutritious, colorful, mouth-watering meal you can. Write a description of it, just as you'd want it to appear in a restaurant menu. If you're really into this, do the *whole* menu. Who knows? You might even convince the family cook (Mom or Dad) to fix that for dinner, with your help, of course.

Suggestion 3: If your family isn't yet up for eating more healthy, ask if you can have your own snack container in the fridge. Fill it with cut-up veggies and fruit so you won't be tempted to just grab a bag of chips when you're hungry and tired. Items that don't have to be kept cold could go in your Mini-Woman Kit—things like low-fat granola bars or whole-grain crackers. If you want to make up snack containers as a group, ask each girl to bring a plastic container and something she can share, like a bunch of celery or a bag of grapes.

Suggestion 4: Become the family chef's apprentice. Ask if you can help in the kitchen—chopping veggies, cutting up fruit, learning how to steam vegetables, and making salads. Eating healthy is more work, so if you're going to suggest that meals be healthier, you'll need to be willing to do some of the tasks involved. For your group activity, ask ahead if your mom will let everyone help her make veggie soup or prepare a salad bar.

Suggestion 5: Have fun helping the cook make things look wonderful before you put them on the table. Could you include a sprig of parsley on each plate? Arrange the cherry tomatoes in a design on top of the salad? Pour the milk in pretty glasses and fold the napkins? As a group, give everyone a decorating task. If that won't work at your house, draw what you think would be a gorgeous table.

That's What I'm Talkin' About

It's really important that you have a good relationship with food, just the way you have a relationship with your BFF. Thinking these things through and discussing them with God will help you get there. As always, you can either fill in your answers here or you can write/draw them in a special notebook.

Do I think of food as my friend or my enemy (or tempter!)? _____

_____.

When I eat unhealthy food, I feel _____

_____ about myself.

Sometimes I eat when I'm not really even hungry because _____

_____.

I don't hang out with people who are bad for me, so when it comes to food that's bad for me, _____

_____

_____.

God, I really need your help with this about my eating habits: _____

_____.

7

The Clean Scene

Most mini-women don't sit around talking about their body odors. I mean, really! But once I get the conversation going, all *kinds* of issues come up:

> I had gym at my co-op, and when I got into my dad's truck, he said, in FRONT of my brothers, 'Girl, did you put deodorant on?' They, of course, all had to comment. AWKWARD!

> One day my brothers came into the family room where I was watching TV and they were all, 'Ewwww! What is that SMELL?' Um, it was my feet ...

> **My friend tells me sometimes that my breath stinks and my mom says the same. When I blow on my hand, I almost faint, so I guess it's a problem.**

Those bring-on-the-puberty hormones we've been talking about? They not only change the way your body looks and functions, but they also change the way it *smells*. Lovely, huh? One odiferous day you discover that you have ...

- *general body odor*, what some people refer to as BO.
- *underarm odor*, body odor's favorite breeding place
- *stinky feet*, with a distinct aroma all their own
- *funky breath*, which is lunch plus bacteria

Who, ME?

When did YOU last notice something about the way you smelled?

_____

_____

_____

Why now, when you already have bras and periods and hairy legs to think about? Let's find that out—and more—because of all the changes that are happening to you, this one is the easiest to deal with.

> It was after PE and I literally radiated sweat onto anything and anyone around me. My armpits soaked my shirt and, you guessed it, people kept their distance from me because I STUNK. Good thing PE is at the end of the day!

Who, ME?

On a sweat scale of drippy to dry, where do YOU fit in?

_____

Who, ME?

What was the last commercial or ad you saw that said you were a loser if you smelled a certain way?

_____

HERE'S THE DEAL ABOUT SMELLY BODIES

The same hormones that are changing your shape are also increasing the amount of sweat your sweat glands produce, and—with millions of those little glands in your body—that can be a lot of perspiration when you're hot, active, or nervous. Sweat is actually a good thing because when it evaporates, your skin cools down, and it removes toxins (icky stuff) from your body.

Good or not, sweat can create a smelly situation.

- Special sweat glands in your underarms and between your legs become active for the first time during puberty.

- It isn't the sweat itself that causes that less than delicious aroma; it's the bacteria living on your skin that break down the sweat and cause an odor.

- Those little critters really like the sweat in your armpits and **genital** (between your legs) area. It's warm and dark in those places, perfect conditions for bacteria to enlarge their families.

The obvious question—which a lot of tween girls ask me—is: **What do I DO about it?** It's actually pretty simple:

- Ignore commercials and magazine ads that say pit odor will ruin your life! If somebody doesn't want to be your friend because you're a little stinky between horseback riding and the shower, she needs to take a whiff of her own self! *Everybody* perspires.

- Take a bath or shower every day (maybe every other day in winter if you live in a cold climate) to wash off bacteria. Pay special attention to those breeding areas.

- If you've taken a shower in the morning and you get sweaty during the day, at least wash your pits before you hang out with people again.

- Wear clean clothes. Bacteria hang out on fabric that hasn't made it to the laundry. If you tend to sweat a lot, wear clothes that "breathe," like 100 percent cotton. It absorbs more moisture and lets air circulate, which helps keep you dry.

- If you don't like the way your armpits smell, use a **deodorant**, which covers up the body odor with a nice scent of its own, or an **antiperspirant**, which cuts down on the amount of sweat you produce. Be sure, of course, to wash under your arms before you apply either one.

- If your genital area has an unfamiliar odor, *do not use a feminine hygiene spray*. It can cause irritation. If you wash every day and wear clean cotton underwear, that area shouldn't smell. If it does, you might have an infection, so talk to your mom.

If your armpits turn dark gray or black (and it's your skin, not hair, that's darkening your underarms), you might have a buildup of dry skin from antiperspirants and shaving. Try a lotion that has **lactic acid** for six weeks. If that doesn't help, your dark armpits could be genetic (which means the pigmentation runs in the family), or you could have high insulin levels (especially if you're also dark around your neck, waistline, knuckles, or elbows). A doctor can give you a bleaching cream or check your insulin levels. If you're self-conscious, don't go sleeveless until you get it cleared up—but remember that it's nothing to be ashamed of.

66 Music and a bubble bath. That's heaven. 99

159

> 66 I always clean my shin guards after field hockey or soccer because they are STINK-Y!!! 99

> 66 I am practically OCD about using lots of deodorant! 99

Just So You Know

No one is quite sure whether the aluminum in under-arm products is safe for you, so if you want to be extra careful, choose a deodorant without aluminum or an antiperspirant with "buffered aluminum sulfate." There is NO evidence that using either one causes cancer.

> 66 I forgot deodorant on a day when I had four back-to-back dance classes. The last one was ballet, and I got stuck standing by the window, and let me inter-ject here that summers in Texas are REALLY hot, so being by the glass with the sun beating against it was torture. It also happened to be on a day we had a substitute that I really like and I wanted her to come over and give me corrections, but I was so afraid she would stay away from me because of the smell. 99

> 66 I love, love, LOVE an oatmeal bath! It's good for your skin too. 99

> **Before** I started wearing deodorant, one day my dad said, right out of the blue, 'You stink.' So my mom got some deodorant from the bathroom and taught me how to put it on. Right in front of the whole family. It was the most embarrassing thing that ever happened to me. **""**

Just So You Know

If armpit odor is making you self-conscious and you've grown hair under your arms, shaving will help stop bacteria from taking up residence. Discuss that with your mom and read chapter 14 about hair removal.

HERE'S THE DEAL ABOUT STINKY FEET

Feet can create a special brand of yuckiness, especially if you spend most of your day in tennis shoes and socks. If you gag when you kick off your tennies, here are some easy remedies:

- Be sure your feet are clean before you put on your socks and shoes.

- Sprinkle baby powder, talcum powder, or special foot powder inside your shoes or socks.

- Wear clean cotton or wool socks. Natural fibers will absorb the sweat instead of leaving it on your feet.

- Wear shoes made of natural materials like leather or

canvas, which will let your feet breathe. Try to avoid plastic footwear.

- If your current shoes are giving off a smell, sprinkle baking soda in them at night and then shake them out in the morning. If that doesn't do the job, try a special product like Odor Eaters. Still no luck? Buy new shoes!

- Wear shoes other than tennies when you can.

- Don't stress out if your feet are a little smelly; human beings are, after all, supposed to smell like people!

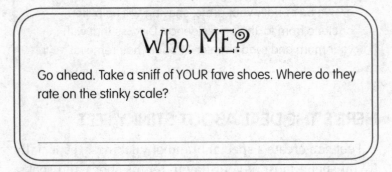

Who, ME?

Go ahead. Take a sniff of YOUR fave shoes. Where do they rate on the stinky scale?

HERE'S THE DEAL ABOUT BAD BREATH

There was nothing sweeter than that sweet baby-girl-friend breath you used to have, even when you first woke up. Now, well, not so much. No worries, though. Just add these steps to your clean routine.

- Brush your teeth twice a day—in the morning and at night. It doesn't hurt to give them a touch-up if you're sprucing up to go out to supper or to a friend's for a birthday party.

- Floss your teeth at least once a day. Yeah, it takes time you'd rather be using for something else, so do it while you're reading a book or watching a movie. It cuts down on **plaque**, which gathers bacteria on your teeth (and you already know the ick-factor of bacteria).

- Rinse with mouthwash after you brush to kill the germs you don't need; again, they're the culprits that cause icky odors.

> When my friend told me right out: 'Your breath stinks,' it wasn't so much embarrassing as it was just rude of her.

- Strong-smelling foods like onions and garlic stay on your breath. If you can't brush your teeth after that Italian dinner or burger with the big ol' onion slice, rinse with water, eat an apple, or suck on a breath mint. If you can't do any of those, don't worry about it. Bad breath is not death to your social life, no matter what the commercials might tell you.

- If you still have breath issues after all of that, ask your dentist about it the next time you visit (which you should do every six months). The doc can tell if you need a prescription mouthwash or if you might have something else going on in your body—which is very rare, so don't freak out!

66 I have super bad breath, and my mom says eating yogurt helps, so I eat it like, all the time. 99

Just So You Know

Although they don't fall into the could-smell-bad category, nails, hair, and skin need more care now that you're on your way to womanhood. The second half of this book will talk about how to keep those parts of you clean.

GOT GOD?

God made our bodies full of sweat glands and hormones and pits and cavities for bacteria to set up housekeeping. So, you may ask, why do we have to worry about being odor-free? Don't we smell the way we're supposed to?

Here's the thing: God doesn't tell us to *worry* about it. Advertisers—who want to sell soap, deodorant, foot spray, and mouthwash—they're the ones who tell us we need to get rid of every human smell so we'll be liked by everyone. They're the ones who want us to stress out.

God just wants us to be clean.

In the book of Leviticus, which was the handbook of rules for the Israelites when they were traveling through the wilderness to the Promised Land, there are six chapters about "the clean" and "the unclean."

- Chapter 11 talks about food.

- Chapter 12 tells women how to be purified after they have a baby.

- In chapters 13 and 14, you can find out everything you ever wanted to know about skin diseases and mildew.

- Need to find out about unclean "discharges"? The answers are in chapter 15.

God provided all of that for two reasons:

- God wanted people to live long and healthy lives. Naturally, then, God taught them about rotten food and other things that would make them sick.

- God wanted them to think about him in absolutely everything they did—even in the way they washed their hands and tidied their tents.

God still wants the same thing for us.

- God wants us disease-free, without a bunch of bacteria taking over our bodies. If we're sick, we can't do what he's put us here to do.

- God still wants us to live lives that are all about him

and his love. One of the loveliest ways to do that is to cleanse our bodies and present our best selves before him, just as the Israelites did.

- While we're thinking about being clean on the outside, God hopes we'll think *a lot* about cleaning up our act on the inside. In fact, God reminds us throughout the Bible, with verses like this:

> The one who has clean hands and a pure heart ...
> will receive blessing from the Lord.
>
> Psalm 24:4–5

Just being scrubbed of every speck of dirt and deodorized from every smell isn't all that God wants. It's the cleanness of our very selves—what we believe and what we do—that really counts.

So while you're taking a shower or sprinkling baking soda in your tennis shoes, look *inside* yourself too and bathe away that desire to flush your little brother down the toilet and scrub out the need to be more popular than Miss Thing over there. When your true self is shining, who cares about a little soccer sweat?

● ●

That Is SO Me!

Don't worry. I'm not going to ask you to choose teams and sniff at each other like puppies! Just think about each of these basic hygiene habits, and put a check next to the ones you're already doing. (And, no, you are not a pig if you end up with very few check marks!)

○ I take a bath or shower every day.

○ I actually use soap when I take a bath or shower!

○ I wear clean clothes every day.

○ I brush my teeth twice a day.

○ I floss my teeth once a day.

○ I rinse with mouthwash at least once a day.

○ I use a deodorant or antiperspirant because I've noticed my underarms are a little rank.

○ I wear cotton or wool socks.

○ I wear cotton underwear.

○ I clean my tennis shoes when they smell.

○ I talk to my mom or another adult I trust when I have odors I can't get rid of.

○ I'm kind about other people's odor issues—like, don't hold my nose when someone has knock-you-down breath.

○ I just let it go if I'm smelly and can't do anything about it right then.

○ I pay as much attention to keeping my inside self clean as I do my outside self.

Now look back at the items you *didn't* check. You can use the information in this chapter to help you with those. This next section will make that more fun—because staying clean doesn't have to be one more chore.

YOU CAN DO IT

All this stuff you have to do all of a sudden can seem like too much. The best approach is to start with one small thing, make that a habit, and then add another small thing. You can do that with your sisterhood or by yourself with your Mini-Woman Kit—or both. Whatever you do, you're gonna come out smelling like a rose.

Creating a Sisterhood, Part 6

1. When you get the mini-women together this time, get the gathering place smelling good. A bowl of potpourri or a scented candle (with Mom's permission) or some lovely smelling flowers will do the job. A nice aroma can put everybody in a relaxed mood.

2. Get the conversation going with the "Who, ME?" features in this chapter. You can also read the quiz out loud and let everybody answer in their heads.

3. Between the good smells and the laughter, the group will probably be ready to share some of their embarrassing odor moments. Prepare for more giggles.

4. Then get the questions out there, and use this chapter to answer them together.

5. Do steps 1–3 under "Your Mini-Woman Kit" together. (See next page.)

6. Decide how you're going to support each other in steps 4–6. You're getting pretty good at this now, right?

7. Include prayer, of course. It may seem a little strange

to be praying that Susie-Q will feel more comfortable about her armpits, but God is in the details!

Your Mini-Woman Kit, Part 6

What you're doing:

- Taking the first small step in developing some new habits to go with your changing body. Once you begin to do it almost without thinking about it, you'll be ready for the next new habit, and the next, until staying healthy and clean will just be part of who you are.

What you'll need:

- this chapter
- fun Post-it Notes, index cards, or small slips of paper
- your fave markers or pens

How to make it happen:

1. Choose one item under "That Is SO Me!" that you did NOT check off. A good choice is the thing you're most self-conscious about.

2. Make a list of supplies you'll need to begin dealing with that particular odor issue. Example: For dealing with underarm odor, I'll need:

   - soap or body wash
   - washcloth or loofah

- a deodorant or antiperspirant (without aluminum) I like the smell of

3. Using your Post-its, index cards, or small paper, create a fun reminder for yourself with pens or markers. If you're going to keep it in a "public" place like the family bathroom, you can do it in code or just draw a picture (to ward off brotherly jokes at your expense). If you're going to tuck it into your kit, it'll be fun to make it match all the other lovely stuff you've put in there.

4. Place your reminder where it will, well, remind you! A reminder to use mouthwash could go inside the medicine cabinet. Put a note to sprinkle baby powder in your socks in your sock drawer.

5. A new task usually becomes a habit after two weeks, so place a tiny mark or star on your reminder note each day that you use your deodorant or sprinkle your tennies or gargle with that mouthwash.

6. When you have fourteen tiny marks, choose another unchecked item from the quiz, gather your supplies, and make a new reminder. One step at a time—that's how we make our lives better.

That's What I'm Talkin' About

While you're doing all this, you're becoming a responsible young woman who doesn't sit around and whine about how much trouble it is to grow up. YOU take on your new tasks like the mature person you are. YOU are ready for some of the good parts of growing up, like having more choices. This is a good time to think about all that and chat with God about it.

As always, you can either fill in your answers here or you can write/draw them in a special notebook.

I'm feeling like all the different things I need to do to keep clean are _____

_____

_____.

I can sort of feel a change in my attitude about my body in this way _____

_____.

Do I feel more grown up now that I'm paying attention to things like the way I smell? _____

_____.

About the balance between my outside and my inside, I think I'm _____

_____.

8

That Whole Boy Thing

Boys. A year or two ago, they were just absurd little creeps. Annoying, but not really a problem if you kept your distance. Then, your fellow mini-women tell me, things started to change.

"There's this one guy and I think I have a crush on him. I think he looks handsome and is nice, not like most other boys I've met. Only I don't know what to do with that."

"I have some friends who are boys, and they're great. They always crack me up, and there isn't as much drama as there is with girls. But my girlfriends keep saying I 'like' those guys and I'm 'going out with them.' What is UP with that?"

"There's a guy I'm really good friends with and our families are friends, but lately all he ever tells me is that I look nice and I'm a good dancer and I have a pretty smile, which is really sweet of him, but it's kind of awkward because I feel like we can't have normal conversations anymore."

"People are pairing up and they're only twelve! I never had and never will have a boyfriend. Period. Ewww."

Who, ME?

Put a check mark next to the quote above that makes YOU think, "That's me!"

It might not seem like confusion about boys has anything to do with puberty, but, oh, it does. You can blame those hormones—or thank them! Before we go there, though, let's look to see how all of this is a God-thing.

• •

GOT GOD?

The same hormones God puts into action so you can have babies cause you to be attracted to guys so you'll *want* to have their kids. Of course, that wasn't such a big deal back in biblical times (and even up until about a hundred years ago), when girls didn't reach puberty until they were fourteen and then got married not long after. In today's world, you're more likely to start puberty at age ten and not get married until you're in your twenties. That's more than a decade!

That's why it's really important to know what God wants when it comes to you and boys. Otherwise, all those feelings that come with liking a boy's attention can get tangled up. There are things from the Bible we know for sure.

> That is why a man leaves his father and mother and is united to his wife, and they become one flesh.
>
> Genesis 2:24

- God set it up from the very beginning that men and women are supposed to be partners and become like one person, not just in body, but in building a life together. He definitely made it so men and women would be attracted to each other. The minute Adam laid eyes on Eve, he said, "This is now bone of my bones and flesh of my flesh" (Genesis 2:23).

- Then God set up a simple guideline to protect a couple when they decide to spend their lives together. "You shall not commit adultery" (Exodus 20:14). It's one of the Ten Commandments, the rules for living, and it means, "Don't do married-people stuff with somebody you're not married to." If your parents haven't already talked to you about the special physical things a husband and wife do together, which can be the start of a baby, it's up to you whether you want to ask them about that. It will be a special conversation that'll explain a lot about the purpose of puberty. For now, just know that God makes it clear and simple: save those special things for marriage.

- After puberty takes hold, your body and mind will want to take you close to the cute boy who makes you feel special. There's nothing wrong with the desire itself; that's how God made you. The challenge is not to let it tell you what you're going to do. Whole books have been written about **purity**—which is what we're talking about here—and you'll probably read some of them as you get older. You'll definitely hear a lot about it when you're a teenager. Right now, though, is a good time to fill your mind and heart with something that will make the challenge easier for you as boys grow cuter to you and become less absurd and creepy. That something is God's "*whatever.*"

> Whatever is true, whatever is noble, whatever is right, whatever is pure, whatever is lovely, whatever is admirable—if anything is excellent or praiseworthy—think about such things. Whatever you have learned or received or heard from me, or seen in me—put it into practice. And the God of peace will be with you.
>
> Philippians 4:8–9

Who, ME?

What question do YOU have about the whole boy thing?

_____

_____

> I'm a tomboy and I guess I get along better with the male species than the female.

> I've been friends with this one boy for, like, ever and he knows I'd beat the living daylights out of him if he tried to flirt with me, so he doesn't.

Who, ME?

What guy do YOU know who you'd like to be just friends with?

_____

One mini-woman wrote this to me:

"The boy thing takes up my life! Seriously, I can't focus at school, home, or anything anymore because all I'm thinking about is him!!! It's horrible. My grades are going down. I've always been straight A's, and now I'm getting B's. My parents think I'm sick or something."

That's not a boy-place you want to be. If you're feeling like this fellow tween girl does, it's probably because …

- you're not getting enough attention where you really need it.

- you're thinking of yourself as only being "good enough" if a boy likes you.

Talk to a grown-up you trust who can help you figure out what's going on and get you back to a healthy place where boys are concerned. They're part of your life, but they should never be ALL of it!

HERE'S THE DEAL WITH YOU AND TWEEN BOYS

You don't have to go hide in an all-girl school until you're ready to get married. The tween years are a good time to get to know what boys are like. (Because they are *so* different from girls—or haven't you noticed?) Let's take a look at some of the boy-girl relationships you might experience before your teen years.

○ **Having boys as friends**—Boys can make really good pals because they don't tend to gossip and get jealous of your other friends—you know, the kind of stuff girls do (which you can read about in *Girl Politics*).

• A guy friend is fun to have adventures with, and he can explain a lot about the boy world.

• **The challenge**: Other kids might tease you about "going out" and assume you're boyfriend and girl-friend. **Whatever.** Explain that you're just friends and then ignore the comments. You and your friend-who's-a-boy should talk about the teasing and rumors so you don't start feeling weird with each other.

○ **Having a crush on a boy**—A crush is when you have a romantic feeling about a boy. Maybe you daydream about him, wondering what it would be like to be his girlfriend. Just catching a glimpse of him or saying hi to him might make you smile for hours.

- It's like private practice for the time when you really will fall in love with somebody. It feels exciting.

- **The challenge**: You find yourself mooning over somebody who doesn't notice you or is even rude to you. That can be painful, but it doesn't mean you aren't precious and wonderful. It's just one of those little emotional things that will go away quickly. If the sad feelings last for more than a day, talk to an adult you trust. It's just way too soon for you to be that affected by a boy; there is probably something else going on with you that you don't even realize.

○ **Having a crush on an older or famous guy**—It isn't unusual to have fluttery feelings about a handsome male teacher or your church youth director with the great personality. Or to daydream about meeting that music star, actor, or major athlete you think is amazing.

- That kind of daydreaming is healthy, because it's a safe way to enjoy those feelings without ever having to worry about what to do with them. Besides, those guys aren't as, well, flawed as the guys you actually know. Again, it's a way of mentally rehearsing for the time when you'll have a real romance.

- **The challenge**: Your larger-than-life crush may disappoint you by doing something unforgivable like getting married (!) or committing some huge mistake that makes the news. Since you didn't have an actual relationship with this person, your bummed-out feeling will go away, but it prepares you for the guys in your future who may let you down. They are, after all, only human.

○ **"Going out" with a boy**—At this point in your life, you really aren't going to "go" anywhere with a boy, since you can't drive and your parents are SO not going to let you start dating! But even kids in elementary school will use that phrase to let people know they're boyfriend and girlfriend and that their feelings are only for each other. At least for today.

- Most of the time that means they pass notes or smile at each other across the room, and they will very likely "break up" before the day is over. As long as it's just a happy game, it's another one of those practice runs for the future.

- **The challenge**: Kids (usually the girls) can take it too seriously and get into jealous fights with each other or feel totally devastated when the "breakup" happens. It's also not healthy when girls get so wrapped up in having a "boyfriend" that they can't talk or think about anything else, and they start changing themselves to get boys to like them. In fact, that's never healthy, no matter how old you are. Since there's really no future in "going out" at this age, why complicate your life? There's too much fun to be had doing other healthier things.

> ❝I guess it's weird to like this celebrity guy who doesn't even know I live! It's just fun, and it's not like I'm obsessing or something.❞

> ❝Why do guys always act like idiots when they're trying to get you to like them? Once this boy that everybody said liked me came up to me and said my memory was a peanut. I still have no idea what he meant.❞

Who, ME?

Have YOU ever daydreamed about meeting a male star?

_____

_____

_____

Just So You Know

In one study of over a thousand tweens, nearly half of eleven- to fourteen-year-olds said they had had what they considered to be boyfriends or girlfriends. Their main means of communication with each other? Texting.

One girl reported exchanging 300 text messages a day with her "boyfriend."

66 To me when kids my age talk about 'going out,' that means they're a couple who will break up soon. **99**

66 To me, all that going out means is a guy knows you like him and you know he likes you. **99**

66 There was this one boy that I liked, and I wouldn't look at him or talk to him because I thought then he would know that I liked him. Then my brother said that if I'm doing that, then he probably knows that I like him. In these cases, I'm glad I have a brother! **99**

Who, ME?

Where do YOU stand on crushes?

_____

_____

_____

66 Sometimes I wonder what it would be like to have a boyfriend, but I don't really WANT one. **99**

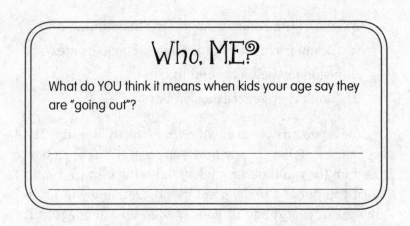

Who, ME?

What do YOU think it means when kids your age say they are "going out"?

_____

_____

> I used to be completely boy crazy, and I had probably ten crushes before I was ten. Right now there's this one boy, and every time he says my name, I get this warm, happy feeling. All of my friends think he's awful, and my brain agrees, but my heart isn't with the program. However, I know he's a Christian and he's my age, so when I'm much, much, much, much older, I wonder if I'll ever date him.

That Is SO Me!

You probably already know where you are with the guy thing, so instead, let's look at how you might handle some boy-related situations. Let this "quiz" be a fun way to learn about the sometimes-weird world of dealing with males.

1. If I have a crush on a boy in my class, I

    a. tell him how I feel.

b. ignore him so he won't know I like him.

c. ask my friend to ask his friend if he likes me.

d. just enjoy being around him.

e. I don't ever get crushes on boys.

Unless you answered **e**, which is perfectly fine, **d** is the best choice. Telling a boy how you feel (**a**) might embarrass him (or **you** if he says yuck). Ignoring him (**b**) might cheat you out of a really good friend. Option **c** will probably mean everybody in your grade will know about it within ten minutes (even if you've sworn everybody to secrecy).

2. If a boy likes me and I'm not interested in being his girlfriend (even for an hour), I

a. don't really say yes or no and hope he'll figure it out.

b. get my friend to tell him to back off.

c. tell him I can't stand him so he'll leave me alone.

d. tell him straight out that I'll be his friend but not his girlfriend.

e. I don't think a boy has ever had a crush on me.

Unless you answered **e**, which again is perfectly healthy, **d** is the best approach. That way, you may find a really good friend, but you don't have to go through all that dramatic stuff. Hoping he'll figure it out (**a**) isn't really fair, even though it's hard to disappoint someone. Getting friends to tell him (**b**) is a little cowardly and isn't a good habit to get into. Option **c** is downright mean and SO isn't you.

3. If a boy teases me and drives me nuts, I

   a. think he has a crush on me.

   b. ask my teacher to make him stop.

   c. ignore him.

   d. laugh and tease him back.

   e. Boys don't tease me.

Unless you answered **e**, which makes your life easy (!), all of the other answers are possibly right. Thinking he has a crush on you (**a**) makes sense because boys your age often tease as a way of showing they like you. Go figure! Telling the teacher (**b**) is the best approach if his teasing is mean and threatening. If he's really making you uncomfortable, by all means report it to a grown-up. Ignoring him (**c**) can work because when someone teases, it's usually to get a reaction from you; if you don't give one, there's no point in his continuing. If he doesn't stop and it's interfering with your schoolwork or your security, go to option **b**. Laughing and teasing back (**d**) is a good choice if the teasing is fun and you enjoy the boy and you can join in happily and easily. This could be the start of a great friendship!

4. If all my friends like boys and they try to push me into the boy thing, I

   a. joke about it and hope they get the message, since I don't want to make them mad.

   b. say I like a boy, just to get them to leave me alone.

   c. yell at them to back off.

   d. tell them I'm not ready for boys yet.

   e. That's never happened to me.

Hopefully your answer is **e**, because friends shouldn't put each other in that kind of position. If your answer is **d**, you are right on. It's always best to be honest about how you feel. Joking about it (**a**) leaves the door open for more pushing. Saying you like a boy when you don't (**b**) is just, well, lying and could make things **way** complicated. And option **c**, though it's honest, could put your friendship in danger. There's really never any reason to scream at your friends, and that usually happens only when you let a problem go on for too long without speaking up.

"My friendship with a guy is really interesting because mostly we exchange good-natured insults and compete with each other and have private running jokes."

Just So You Know

Okay to do if it's okay with your parents …

- Go to dances where everybody dances with everybody.
- Go to parties where there are girls AND boys and everybody stays together.
- Go to movies in big groups of guys and gals.

Not okay to do (because it's too much responsibility for you right now) …

- Have somebody's parents drop you off at the movies with a girlfriend to meet with boys there.
- Text your crush secretly after lights-out.
- Stay at a boy-girl party where there's no adult supervision.

HERE'S THE DEAL WITH INAPPROPRIATE THINGS

Since your body is yours (and God's), you have absolute authority over who touches it and how they touch it and who doesn't touch it—even if you're only eight years old. That means that if anyone—ANYONE—touches you in a way that is uncomfortable for you, especially in your private areas ...

- Tell an adult you trust **immediately**.

- Don't worry about whether you're going to get in trouble—you're **not** because it isn't your fault.

- Don't worry that the person is going to get in trouble. He (or she) **will** and **should**, but that isn't your fault either.

Just So You Know

There's a difference between **flirting** with a boy and just being **friendly**.

Flirting: doing things to get attention from a boy because, well, it feels good to get attention. It can be just harmless fun, but be sure to show the person respect and be sure you don't see yourself as just a girl who's good at getting guys to like her.

Being friendly: acting around a boy just as you would around a girl you want to be friends with. It's about knowing them, not about making yourself feel special for five seconds.

- Even if the person threatens that you'll be hurt if you tell anyone, don't believe it. Tell anyway. That's your best protection against being touched that way again.

- It doesn't matter if it's a boy in your class, a relative, an adult you know, or a stranger. If someone touches you in a way you don't want to be touched, it's wrong. Report it at once.

Talk that makes you uncomfortable is just as bad as touching because it makes you feel bad about yourself. That includes ...

- jokes about sexual things, especially if they contain bad language.

- teasing about private things, like how big your breasts are or whether you're having your period.

- suggestions that you do things you know are totally wrong.

- pressure to do those things.

Whether a guy (or girl) says stuff like that to you in person, on the phone, in a text, on Facebook, in an e-mail, or in a chat room it's **sexual harassment** and you should ...

- Tell the person you're offended.

- Stop having anything to do with that person.

- If it doesn't stop, tell an adult you trust; this isn't tattling, it's responsible telling so you can have the freedom to go your way without worrying what's going to be said to you.

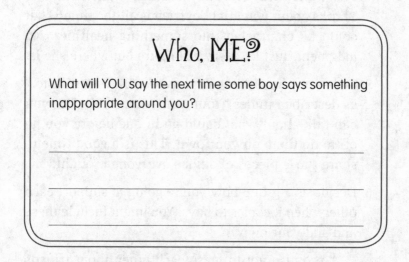

Just So You Know

The average girl your age sees 40,000 commercials a year on TV. That's 666 hours' worth, and 466 of those hours show people looking and acting sexy over things like cars, deodorant, and frozen dinners! That can affect your thinking about how you're going to use your own body.

Who, ME?

What will YOU say the next time some boy says something inappropriate around you?

_____

_____

_____

YOU CAN DO IT

Whether the girls in your sisterhood have just begun to notice that boys aren't always annoying little pests, or you've got some full-blown boy-crazy members, or you're somewhere in between, the topic of boys is likely to get everybody involved.

1. Get together in a male-free space. Ask each girl ahead

of time to bring advice she's gotten about boys, especially from her dad or other important male grown-up in her life.

2. Agree that your conversation isn't going to be about "rating" particular boys on a cuteness scale.

3. Instead, do the quiz together or the Who, ME? boxes.

4. Let each girl get clear on where she is right now in terms of boys. Still thinks they have cooties? That's okay. Has some boy buddies? That's great too. Thinks about potential boyfriends all the time? That could be channeled into something healthier. No judgment. Just let every girl figure out where she **is**.

5. Then you can either each create a "Boy Manifesto," as described under "Your Mini-Woman Kit," or you can talk about what could go in one before you go off to do them on your own. This is a good time to share those pieces of advice everyone brought.

6. Decide as a group how you're going to support each other when it comes to boys. You might include these and add your own …

   ○ A promise not to tease each other about friends who are boys or who likes whom.

   ○ A vow not to gossip about girl-boy relationships.

   ○ A signal to use when one of you is overdoing it with the flirting.

   ○ An agreement to talk about jealousy if it rears its ugly green head.

○ A process for stopping inappropriate talk from boys.

7. If you haven't started praying together yet, now is the perfect time. Girls who pray together about boy issues are most likely to keep those good vows and promises.

Your Mini-Woman Kit, Part 7

Even if you still avoid boys like they have the H_1N_1 virus, this is a good time to decide on your "Boy Manifesto"—which is basically your statement of how you're going to behave around boys. It's way easier to make up your mind about those things before you're suddenly confronted with unexpected feelings.

What you'll need:

○ this book

○ some scratch paper and a pencil or markers

○ some nice paper and a pen

○ the advice you've gathered about boys from wise people—especially your dad (Of all the people in your life, he knows the most about boys and about you at the same time.)

How to make it happen:

1. On the scratch paper, make a list of all the situations you could run into with the male of the species. This chapter has lots. Examples:

- a boy asking me out

- a boy teasing me for fun

- a boy teasing me just to be mean

- a boy wanting to kiss me

- a boy I'm not crazy about following me around

- wanting a boyfriend when everybody else has one and I don't

2. Using this book and the other good advice you've gathered, think about how you'll handle each of those situations. Write them on scratch paper.

3. Write your final polished ideas on your nice piece of paper.

4. For any situation you don't know how to deal with, go to an adult and ask. Then add to your manifesto. Examples:

   - If a boy asks me out before I'm sixteen (or whatever age is set), I will just tell him I don't date yet.

   - If a boy teases me just for fun and it doesn't annoy me, I'll tease back.

   - If a boy teases me to be mean, I'll tell him I thought he was better than that and walk away.

5. If you feel comfortable, show your plan to your parents. Ask them to pray for you. This is the first step in gaining their trust that you're going to handle the whole boy thing in a mature way.

6. Keep your plan in your Mini-Woman Kit so you can refer to it as new situations come up, especially if

you find yourself thinking a lot about that little leaguer that smiled at you.

7. You can also use it to help you pray for wisdom and strength. Chances are, you're gonna need them!

That's What I'm Talkin' About

Now that you have a plan, you won't be caught by surprise. You can relax and enjoy friendships with boys. You know that you know how to make good choices. There's still a lot to talk to God about, and these suggestions might help. As always, you can fill in your answers here or write/draw them in a special book, or even just think about them.

My biggest challenge with boys is _____

_____

_____.

I wish boys would _____

_____

_____.

When it comes to me and boys, my parents _____

_____

_____.

Is it okay with you, God, that I feel _____

_____

_____ ?

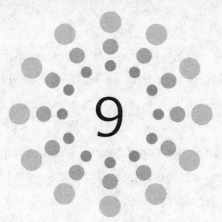

9

Body Bullies

The things we've discussed so far in "Body Talk" are normal parts of growing into a young woman. If all you had to deal with were periods, breasts, body hair, a new shape, and the unfamiliar thought that boys might not be poison ivy after all, I could say, "You have nothing to worry about, mini-women!"

Except ... that isn't the way it is. There are some issues that *shouldn't* be part of your life—or anybody's—but they're there in your face just when you already have a long list of changes to cope with. Your fellow tween girls voice those concerns:

> It's sad to me that lots of people who were once kids like me turn to drugs and alcohol for 'happiness.'

> 66 I've seen kids not that much older than me get on drugs and then they do not-very-nice things to other people. So then everybody's messed up by it. 99

> 66 I could name about twenty illegal drugs: the street names, categories, and effects. We had to learn them for an exam in school. I don't see how anyone would take them once they've heard about all that, but they still do. 99

I wish you didn't have to think about what I consider to be "body bullies" right now. Things like:

- taking illegal drugs
- drinking alcohol
- smoking cigarettes or marijuana
- listening to music at dangerously high volumes

Who, ME?

Put a question mark next to anything on that list above YOU haven't been given any information on.

I also wish I could agree with this statement from a mini-woman:

> 66 I've always been homeschooled and only go to church activities and listen to only Christian music and read Christian books. I've never been taught anything about that stuff, and I don't need to be. 99

Wishing doesn't make it so, does it? The items on that list can be very much a part of the world you're going to move into when you get to middle school, if you aren't there already, and it's important that you be prepared rather than surprised. I hope you *will* continue to believe that drugs, alcohol, and smoking are totally bad for you, which is why it's important for you to know more than just the "names, categories, and effects." Please read this chapter because ...

- Between the ages of eight and twelve, you will make key decisions about what you're going to be like and how you're going to act, no matter what the situation.

- In *many* schools, alcohol and tobacco are easy for eleven- and twelve-year-olds to get their hands on. Many kids first experiment with drinking and smoking in fifth and sixth grades, as they figure out who they're going to be and what they're going to do.

- One in every ten kids ages ten through twelve tries drugs (usually marijuana). Girls are equal in number to boys when it comes to becoming addicted (which means having to have more and more).

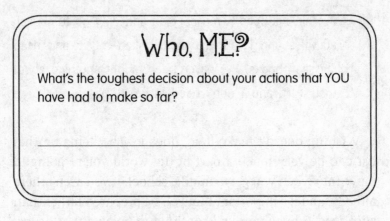

Who, ME?

What's the toughest decision about your actions that YOU have had to make so far?

_____

_____

So, no, it isn't going to be as easy as just saying no. Two things need to happen:

1. You need to have the *facts* about how bad these things are for you.

2. You need to *love* the body, mind, and spirit God has given you so nothing can keep you from respecting and taking care of yourself.

Yeah, this might be the most important chapter in the whole book. Let's start with the facts.

Just So You Know

Smoking ANYTHING is dangerous for you, including crushed up Smarties. (Yes, some kids actually started that trend!)

HERE'S THE DEAL ABOUT SMOKING

1. **It causes lung disease.** And that doesn't just mean sitting around with an oxygen tank when you're old. Even young people can suffer damage **now** from smoking cigarettes.

2. **It's way habit-forming.** Three out of four teen girls who smoke say they've tried to quit and haven't been able to.

3. **It's expensive.** A pack of cigarettes a week costs at least $260 a year (and most smokers go through a lot more than that).

4. **It can cause zits.** Seriously. The nicotine in cigarettes increases the hormones that speed up your body's production of oil, which can clog your pores and cause pimples.

5. **It's a downer.** Girls who smoke are four times more likely to get depressed than girls who don't smoke.

6. **It makes you stupid!** If you're addicted to smoking and you can't have a cigarette (like during a test), your brain doesn't work as well, and your memory isn't as sharp, because you're craving the nicotine in that cigarette.

7. **It makes you lazy.** Smoking makes it harder to exercise, because the tiny air sacs in the lungs are damaged, and you get out of breath more quickly.

8. **It makes you ugly.** It gives you bad breath and smells up your clothes and hair and makes your teeth yellow. Just what every girl wants!

Who, ME?

Can you think of a reason why YOU would want to smoke?

_____

_____

Just So You Know

Studies show that kids between the ages of ten and twelve who don't take a firm stand against smoking are more likely to start smoking if pressured than those who make a solid decision before then. Don't just say maybe. Say no!

> I've mostly just picked up information about drugs and alcohol from here or there or from my older sisters. It's kind of interesting.

Just So You Know

Many people abuse drugs and alcohol because they want to escape their problems. But drinking and doing drugs make it harder, not easier, to deal with your problems. In fact, it creates MORE problems.

> **Some drugs are supposed to make you feel energetic and confident, like speed, but they always have bad consequences, so why not just pray?**

HERE'S THE DEAL ABOUT ALCOHOL AND DRUGS

1. *Alcohol interferes with your growth during puberty.* For example, it steals your body's zinc, which you need to grow strong bones.

2. *Drugs and alcohol destroy brain cells,* which means you can't think as clearly or as quickly. Once those cells are dead, they don't come back to life. And in most cases, your brain doesn't make more.

3. *People who get stoned or drunk risk ...*

   ○ doing something ridiculous and making fools of themselves in front of other people. (It's easy enough to do that when you're NOT drunk!)

   ○ getting physically hurt.

   ○ being influenced to do things they wouldn't dream of doing when they weren't drunk.

   ○ losing friends.

   ○ getting into trouble not only with parents but also with police.

   ○ having their stuff stolen or broken.

   ○ arguing or fighting with people (and possibly being injured).

   ○ throwing up.

○ becoming unconscious.

○ even dying from too much alcohol or a drug over-dose. (In a small, young body, "too much" is not a lot).

4. Besides all that, it's AGAINST THE LAW!

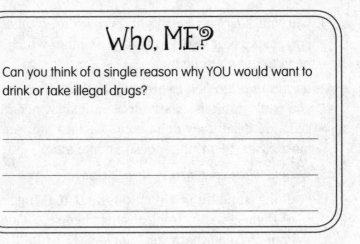

Who, ME?

Can you think of a single reason why YOU would want to drink or take illegal drugs?

_____

_____

_____

Just So You Know

Inhaling household chemicals like glue and paint and shoe polish IS drug abuse, and it's dangerous. They can damage your brain, heart, liver, and kidneys and lead to the use of marijuana, prescription drugs, and harder stuff.

HERE'S THE DEAL ABOUT LOUD MUSIC

Just So You Know

If you're using ear buds and someone standing next to you can hear your music, it's too loud.

You really can experience hearing loss from having your iPod or MP3 player cranked up too high.

- One in five kids ages twelve to nineteen has lost a little bit of hearing because of listening to loud music through earbuds. That's about 6.5 *million* teens and tweens.

- "A little bit" means they can't hear a whisper, rustling leaves, water dripping, or conversations in the cafeteria. It's called **high-frequency hearing loss**.

- Today's young people are listening to music more than twice as long as the generations before you because your digital devices have more battery life and music storage. Hearing loss in teens is thirty percent higher now than it was in the 1980s and 1990s.

- Hearing loss affects your performance in school. Teachers often mistake it for attention deficit disorder (ADD) or a low IQ.

- Hearing loss is permanent.

Just So You Know

Experts say three things will help reduce the danger of hearing loss from personal listening devices:

1. Turn down the volume to sixty percent of full.
2. Take listening breaks. Only use your ear buds for a total of one hour a day and use speakers whenever you can.
3. Use ear protection when you're exposed to loud noises for extended periods of time, like concerts or being around lawn mowers and weed eaters. (If you like numbers, that means noise levels of 110 decibels for more than thirty minutes.)

Who, ME?

Could YOUR volume use some adjusting?

_____

_____

_____

HERE'S THE DEAL ABOUT JUST SAYING NO

So, if all that stuff is obviously bad for you, why does anybody do it? Why don't kids just say no?

It sounds simple, but there are ideas and thoughts that come with—you guessed it—puberty that can make it hard to stay away from drugs, alcohol, and tobacco. It's natural at your age to ...

- want to fit in, be included, and be liked.

- want to do the fun things the other kids are doing.

- want to feel more grown-up.

- want to try new things.

- look up to older kids and role models to show you how to act.

- realize it's *your* body and *you* have control over it (and to think, "So why can't I do whatever I want with it?").

- figure out your body's one of the few things you **do** have control over, when other people are controlling your behavior and your time and where you live.

Who, ME?

Which of those situations sounds most like one YOU might have trouble with?

_____

_____

_____

Just think about these situations:

- ALL the girls at the sleepover are going to try half a glass of somebody's dad's wine, just to see what it tastes and feels like. These are the girls you hang out with all the time. There's nobody else to be with at school. Without them, you'll be all alone in the cafeteria and on the playground.

- At home, your parents treat you like *such* a baby. Your best friend's big sister offers you a cigarette, telling you that you're way more mature than even some of her friends. Just for a minute you'd like to feel grown-up.

- That boy all your friends are giggling about—the most popular kid in the whole class—has marijuana in his backpack, and you see it. If you tell on him, everybody is going to be mad at you. Your life will be over—or it might as well be.

It isn't as easy as it sounds, is it? That's why it's a good thing we've got God.

"One of the things I really like about myself is that I'm headstrong (not in a bad way), like I'm not afraid to go somewhere public and tie my camera to a tree and sing to it in order to make a music video. After doing that, simply walking away from a few friends who are into bad stuff is easy."

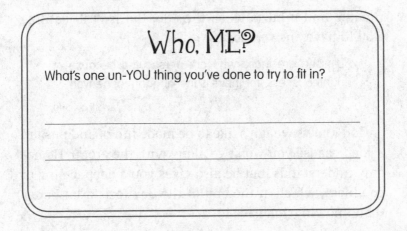

Who, ME?

What's one un-YOU thing you've done to try to fit in?

_____

_____

_____

GOT GOD?

The reason friends are so important to you right now is because God set it up that way. It's part of the natural growing-up process for you to start to turn your attention away from your family and focus it on your friends. You will someday move out of your parents' house completely to have your own life, and right now you are slowly learning how.

Your friends are giving you the safe, secure feeling of belonging that came totally from your family when you were a small girl. But what if suddenly you won't belong if you don't do what your friends are doing? What if they're making choices you know aren't right or healthy? What if you wind up alone and outcast and never have friends again and everyone hates you and—

Okay, you can stop right there, because you _know_ that last one isn't going to happen! The other things can, though, and it hurts when they do. But isn't it just like God to have answers for us?

> Blessed are those who are persecuted because of righteousness, for theirs is the kingdom of heaven.
>
> Matthew 5:10

God knows what it's like to be made fun of and pushed aside because you won't go along with the group. He not only understands, but he also gives you a deep feeling of goodness, which at the end of the day feels a lot better than knowing you gave in.

> Do not envy the wicked,
> do not desire their company;
> for their hearts plot violence,
> and their lips talk about making trouble.
>
> Proverbs 24:1–2

It can be painful, but some friendships do break up in these tween years over different ideas about what's right and what's wrong. The girls you always played dolls with and swam and went to Brownies with may make choices about their lives that you can't agree with. Then it's time to end the friendship. Go ahead and cry, and then be glad you're free from things that are only going to get you into trouble.

> [Peter said,] "Save yourselves from this corrupt generation." … All the believers were together and had everything in common…. Every day they continued to meet together…. They broke bread in their homes and ate together with glad and sincere hearts, praising God and enjoying the favor of all the people.
>
> Acts 2:40, 44, 46–47

Gather new friends, other girls (and even boys) who are making healthy decisions about their lives. Get together to talk about how you're going to resist the bad stuff and fill your time with *great* stuff. Hang out with kids who love God the way you do.

> It is God's will ... that each of you should learn to control your own body in a way that is holy and honorable.... For God did not call us to be impure, but to live a holy life. Therefore, anyone who rejects this instruction does not reject a human being but God ... who gives you his Holy Spirit.
>
> 1 Thessalonians 4:3–4, 7–8

Remember that taking care of your temple is more important than your social life. We're talking about your body, the one you share with God. Appreciate and give dignity to it. If you reject your body by abusing it, you reject God.

Clear enough?

" I think things like drug and alcohol abuse make God sad because we're trying to find our security and worth in places other than him, and he knows that won't bring lasting, true happiness. "

That Is SO Me!

Imagine that you and your friends are at one of your houses and you're going to watch a movie together. There are bunches to choose from. The girl's mom has set out snacks in the kitchen for you, and both parents have gone to bed. Circle *all* the things below that you would do. Remember—be honest!

○ Make sure the kitchen isn't left messy.

○ Pick the movie.

○ Turn the movie off if it's lame.

○ Start the movie.

○ See what's in the pantry to eat.

○ Announce you're hungry.

○ Keep watching as long as everyone else does.

○ See if there's an R-rated movie.

○ Go do something else if the movie's lame.

○ Watch what the group decides.

○ Join in the fun of everyone eating the same thing.

○ Turn the movie off if it has violence or bad language.

Now find all your choices in the following lists. You will probably see yourself in more than one because you're a complex human being. Just let the lists tell you how your choices sometimes serve you well and sometimes don't. What you discover about yourself can help prepare you for bigger choices in the future that can have more serious results.

Rule Maker

- Pick the movie.
- Announce you're hungry.

- Turn the movie off if it's lame.

You're a strong person in your group. You're often the one who decides what's going to happen and how things are going to be done. You can use that to influence your friends to make fun, not trouble. Just be careful not to be too B-O-S-S-Y.

Rule Keeper

- Start the movie.
- Make sure the kitchen isn't left messy.
- Turn the movie off if it has violence or bad language.

You don't make the rules, but you know them and you make sure everybody else does too. Even if they don't stick to them, you will. Keep doing that when it comes to the tough decisions. Just remember that you're not responsible for other people's choices, so you don't always have to be the watchdog.

Rule Follower

- Watch what the group decides.
- Join in the fun of everyone eating the same thing.
- Keep watching as long as everyone else does.

You're an easy person to get along with, and you keep things calm in your group of friends by being agreeable. It's good to be unselfish, but be careful not to follow the group's "rules" if they aren't good ones. Stand up for what's right when you need to.

Rule Breaker

- See if there's an R-rated movie.
- See what's in the pantry to eat.
- Go do something else if the movie is lame.

You are an independent person, and you like to see what all the possibilities are. You aren't afraid to take risks or see how far the rules can be pushed (just in case they're lame rules). Use your adventurous spirit to question your friends when they all just want to go along with the crowd—in the wrong direction. Be sure your choices are brave, not just rebellious.

> I go to an inner-city school, and I know people who SAY they do drugs. It hasn't changed me, though, I think because I pray for them and because I want to help them rather than be like them.

YOU CAN DO IT

Making good choices is so much easier if (a) you and your sisterhood make them together and (b) you have a for-real relationship with God who will nudge you when you start to waver. That's what these activities are all about.

Creating a Sisterhood, Part 7

1. Gather where there's a computer and a printer.

2. Pray as a group that God will show you exactly the right things to decide.

3. Go through this chapter together, and make a list of the issues you'll probably face (or maybe already do). Your list would include things like drinking, smoking, listening to too-loud music, and anything you feel pressured to do that you know isn't a good idea. At all. Leave a few lines between items.

4. Talk about each issue and decide …

   ○ your attitude about it. (Is it wrong? Unhealthy? Disgusting?)

   ○ how you'll resist it. (Run the other way? Refuse to hang out with people who do it? Call each other when you're tempted?)

   ○ how you'll fight it in your world. (Confront kids who do it? Make T-shirts with slogans? Befriend girls who are feeling pressured?)

5. Type up your plan on a computer, and print copies for everyone in your sisterhood, or let each person write out and decorate her own copy while you talk. (And snack, of course!)

6. Pray together again. You might specifically ask God for …

   ○ the maturity to know how real "grown-ups" make decisions.

   ○ the strength to take a stand instead of hoping things don't happen to you.

   ○ the knowledge that you aren't alone in facing the hard things that may lie ahead.

○ the understanding that it's more fun to be healthy with your friends than to mess up your lives together.

Your Mini-Woman Kit, Part 8

Even if you have a sisterhood more solid than your mom's "No!" (and there are few things more solid than that!), the decisions you make are, in the end, *yours*. The only way to make sure they're good ones is to be solid with God too. It might help you to have a solid, hold-in-your-hand way to figure out if a choice is a God-thing.

A Cross for the Crossroads

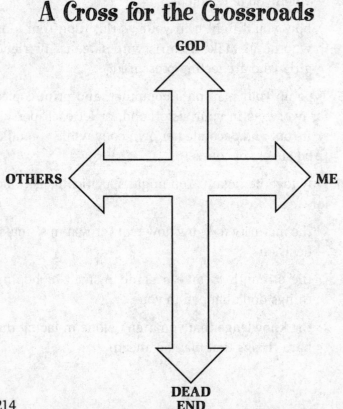

What you'll need:

○ Index card, journal, or other place to draw

○ Markers, colored pencils, or writing utensil of choice

How to make it happen:

1. The best place to create your cross would be on an index card that you could carry with you, put up in your room, on your mirror, on your refrigerator, or any place to see when you need a reminder.

2. Using your markers (or writing utensil of choice), draw a cross, and decorate it any way you'd like.

3. At the top of the cross, draw a little arrow that points up and label it "God."

4. At the bottom of the cross, draw a little arrow that points down and label it "Dead End."

5. Draw an arrow to the left and label it "Others," and an arrow to the right labled "Me."

6. Place your cross in an area so you can see it and be reminded to think about your choices before you make them.

How to use it:

When you're faced with a tough decision, especially one that affects how you're going to treat your body, hold the cross you made in your hand and ask yourself which direction each option would take you.

- OTHERS: Will you do it *just* to please your friends or impress the cool kids? Or would it be a good thing for your BFFs or a good example for someone?

- ME: Will you do it *only* to make yourself feel good? Or will it help you grow?

- DEAD END: Will it lead you nowhere good?

- GOD: Will it make God smile?

It's great to consider other people when you make decisions, and you need to feel good about those choices too. But any action you take should *never* land you in a dead place (hurt, in trouble, grounded for the rest of your life), and it should *always* be an answer God will approve of. If you don't know what that is, just ask him!

That's What I'm Talkin' About

This is big stuff, so it requires more thought than just about anything else you face as a mini-woman. These things-to-ponder-with-God might help you stay clear.

One person who might stand in the way of me making a good decision is _____

_____

_____.

I could deal with that person by _____

_____

_____.

One mistake I make a lot when I'm faced with choices is

_____.

I could start breaking that habit by _____

_____

_____.

Most of the time I try to please _____

_____

and that is (a) a God-thing? Or (b) a Dead End?

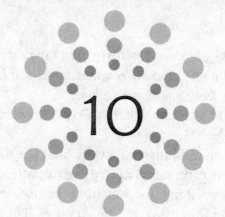

10

Mini-Woman!

Recently I asked the girls on my *Tween You and Me* blog how they want to grow into young women. I thought it might be a confusing question for them, but evidently it wasn't. Here's what a few of them said:

"I feel like a new mini-woman now that I have the support and inspiration and kindness of the girls on this blog. Now I can keep concentrating on God-things and be more and more secure."

"I think I'll use a journal and write down the things I'm scared about and wonder about and get excited about. I want to share more things with my older sisters, but some I think I'd like to do on my own. Like yesterday I went outside at sunset and sat and wrote in my journal about how I just got pimples ..."

"I want to go through puberty with my mom. What else can I say? I want support from her through all of this just like she has been giving me so far."

"I want to grow up holding God's hand, and I never want to let go."

Four different kinds of answers, and yet they all have one thing in common: **They're paying attention to the process**. They aren't just watching themselves grow and kind of muddling through the changes. They're alert to what's going on, and they're taking part in it.

How about you? Now that you have all this information, how do you want to continue along this puberty path and into young womanhood? What you do will be unique to you, but as always, some suggestions that apply to everybody will help you along the way. Where else would we start except with God, right?

- -

GOT GOD?

When God created people, he gave each of us the same special touch:

> God created mankind in his own image,
> in the image of God he created him;
> male and female he created them.

Genesis 1:27

Can you even begin to *think* about the care that went into creating you, a mini-woman? Puberty alone boggles the mind with all its details and the way everything works together.

And what about the way each of us is different? No two of us are exactly alike in body. We are each exactly the way God meant for us to be. Besides just being awesome, that tells you three things that you need to know right now:

1. You can have confidence that God gave you precisely the body you're supposed to have.

2. You've really gotta love that body.

3. You're responsible for taking care of it.

Notice there's no comparing in that description—no "I wish I were as skinny as she is," or "I'm glad I have breasts now, not like Little Flat Chest over there."

Notice there's no self-hate mentioned there—no "I'm so fat I'm going to starve myself," or "Who cares if I exercise? I'm just a blob anyway."

And do you see any shoving the job off on somebody else? There's no "I can't help it if the school cafeteria only serves pizza," or "My family members aren't athletes. We just like to watch TV."

Yeah, it's very clear.

○ Love that precious body.

○ Be sure it's totally you.

○ Take the best care of it that you can.

○ God says so.

Without that, the rest of the info in this book won't help you become the young woman you were meant to be. Believe it, no matter what anybody else may try to tell you.

Got that? Then let's move on to one last look inside yourself.

● ●

That Is SO Me!

Before we move on to our next section, "Beauty Matters," let's just see how you're doing—so you can give yourself a hug—and what you might want to work on next—so you can keep growing into you.

Put a check mark next to each of the things you've done or are doing for body care.

○ I understand what's happening or is about to happen inside my body (puberty).

○ I have a comfortable bra or know what size I wear and what kind I'd like to try.

○ I know I'm right where I should be—not "ahead" or "behind" in my development.

○ I have my supplies ready for when I start my first or next period.

○ I have a Personal Fitness Plan to make sure I get enough exercise.

○ I eat healthy, according to the food pyramid.

○ I get at least eight hours of sleep every night.

○ I refuse to "go on a diet" unless my doctor says I need to.

○ I drink at least six glasses of water a day.

○ I take a bath or shower every day.

○ I wear clean clothes every day.

○ I use a deodorant or antiperspirant if I need to.

○ I have a Boy Manifesto.

○ I have a plan for dealing with "Body Bullies."

○ I have a Sisterhood to go through puberty with.

○ I go to a trusted adult with problems that bother or upset me.

For items you did not check, make a list here of one small thing you can do to change each one. Examples:

○ Ask my dad to shoo me off to bed a half hour earlier.

○ Start asking my mom more questions.

○ Throw away all that leftover Easter (Halloween, Valentine's) candy.

○ _____

○ _____

YOU CAN DO IT

Keep meeting with your sisterhood. Keep sharing good information and supporting each other and praying for each other. If you haven't been able to gather a group of tween girls, please join us on the *Tween You and Me* blog, tweenyouandme.typepad.com. Even if you do have a girl group, we'd still love to have you. You can never have too many fellow mini-women on the journey.

Your Mini-Woman Kit, Part 9

When I asked the girls on the blog to tell how they'd like to grow into young womanhood, they did something without my even suggesting it. They each shared their **life verse**. Here are a few of those:

> "For I know the plans I have for you," declares the Lord, 'plans to prosper you and not to harm you, plans to give you a hope and a future. Then you will call upon me and come and pray to me, and I will listen to you."
>
> Jeremiah 29:11–12

> [Your beauty] should be that of your inner self, the unfading beauty of a gentle and quiet spirit, which is of great worth in God's sight.
>
> 1 Peter 3:4

> The Lord your God will be with you wherever you go.
>
> Joshua 1:9

> Then I heard the voice of the Lord saying, "Whom shall I send? And who will go for us?" And I said, "Here am I. Send me!"
>
> Isaiah 6:8

> I am fearfully and wonderfully made.
>
> Psalm 139:14

"Your will be done."

I can think of no better final (for now, at least!) addition to your Mini-Woman Kit than a life verse, all framed and lovely, to help you remember that no matter how bloated and crampy and cranky and hairy and confused you feel, God has already spoken the words that will not only get you through it but lead you one step further toward that confident, womanly human being you were born to be.

What you'll need:

- ○ a Bible
- ○ a piece of cardboard a little smaller than the inside of the lid of your kit box
- ○ a very YOU piece of fabric or wrapping paper large enough to cover the cardboard
- ○ glue (fabric glue works best on, well, fabric!)
- ○ a piece of plain fabric or paper about an inch smaller than the cardboard on all sides
- ○ markers/pens or fabric paint

How to make it happen:

1. Choose a life verse if you haven't already. The ones listed above are wonderful, and there are, of course, hundreds of others. If you're at a loss, get a Christian you respect to help you find one.

2. Cover the cardboard with the fabric or wrapping paper, and glue it down securely.

3. Write or paint your verse on the plain paper or fabric. You can also do this on your computer, print it out, and then cut the paper down to size.

4. Glue your verse in the center of your covered cardboard. Voilá—framed and ready to place right in your Mini-Woman Kit.

That's What I'm Talkin' About

I hope that as you finish the "Body Talk" part of this book, you've started to form the habit of focusing on your thoughts and questions and struggles by writing them down or drawing them and, of course, discussing them with God. You'll continue to come up with your own "conversation starters," but let's close with one last list from me to you:

I want my walking on the path into young womanhood to be like _____

_____ .

If that's going to happen, I'm going to need to _____

_____ .

From now on, I'm going to pay more attention to _____

_____

_____ .

I still need to get better at these things _____

_____

_____ .

I still want to know _____

_____

_____ .

Part II: Beauty Matters

11

You've Got It Goin' On

You are beautiful.

I'm serious.

This isn't like your mom saying, "**I** think you're beautiful," and you thinking, "You **have** to say that. You're my **mother**!"

This is me, who has never met you, saying, "Miniwoman, you are a work of art" because I know it without even seeing you.

Okay, so maybe you aren't front-cover-of-*Seventeen*-magazine pretty. Maybe grown-ups don't say, "Oh, honey, you are going to break some hearts with those looks when you get older." It may even be that other kids pick apart your appearance until you feel downright ugly.

But I can still say, "You are beautiful."

How is that possible? How can I even *think* about telling you that you're a lovely human being when you're hearing things like *this* practically 24/7?

○ The only way to be pretty is to be skinny.

○ Your skin has to be perfect. You can't have any pimples. At all.

○ You have to tame frizzy hair or you're heinous.

○ You have to keep up with clothes trends or you look stupid.

○ You have to be girly to even be a real girl.

Who, ME?

Draw a small frowny face next to the statements above that YOU have heard, read, or just know from somewhere.

To hear people talk, you'd think the only girls who are worth looking at are drinking-straw-thin with flawless complexions, thick blonde hair and enormous blue eyes, and they dress only in the trends that just started this morning.

That list of lies sneaks up on you from everywhere, right?

- When you're watching **TV**, here come the commercials about diet programs, skin-care products, hair stuff, even special creams to use so your *feet* will be pretty. They make it sound like, "Use this and your life will be perfect. Don't and you'll be miserable."

- When you're flipping through a **magazine** in the orthodontist's office or you get on the **Internet** to do some homework, there are the ads popping up to tell you how to get longer eyelashes and larger breasts and more glamorous fingernails. (Who knew fingernails were *supposed* to be glam? Especially when you're eleven!)

- When you're riding in the backseat of your mom's car and every other **billboard** you pass has a picture of a drop-dead gorgeous woman on a motorcycle or a washing machine or a stack of radial tires. It's enough to make you think, "I'm never going to look like that so why bother to even brush my hair?"

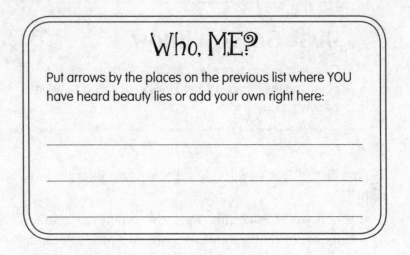

Who, ME?

Put arrows by the places on the previous list where YOU have heard beauty lies or add your own right here:

_____

_____

_____

And those are just the messages the adult world is sending you. The most depressing signals that you aren't model material (and are therefore homelier than a basset hound) can sometimes come from your own peers. Here's what your fellow mini-women have shared with me on the *Tween You and Me* blog:

    ❝I'm twelve and I weigh like 135, but my friends who are in the 90s and low 100s act like I'm way huger than them. I'm tall and I have muscle, but they still think I'm fat.❞

    ❝All my friends are petite and I'm just, like, gangly and tall and awkward. They call me 'klutz' when they're joking around, but it still hurts my feelings.❞

66 I always worry about the way I look. I worry that people won't be friends with me, because some are like that. I just want to look pretty so I can feel good about myself. 99

66 I always play the comparison game. I see people walking around with all these fancy smancy clothes, and they look so much better. Sometimes they make comments that let me know I'm not good enough or fashionable enough. 99

66 I just want to be liked and accepted, and it seems sometimes the only way to do that is to look, well, 'sexy.' And I don't WANT to! 99

66 My problem is that I'm so small for my age. Once someone asked me if I was a dwarf. It was so embarrassing! 99

66 People always make fun of me because I'm half-Filippino, half-American. They say I look weird. 99

The next thing most of those mini-women added was some version of one girl's comment:

> **" I am trying (and kind of failing) to remember that God is only going to look at our hearts. It doesn't matter to him how we look. "**

We all know that, but when some kid calls you "Pizza Face" or "Jabba the Hutt," it's way hard not to look in the mirror and think, "He's right!" Then your prayer is not so much "Thank you, God, for making me just the way I am." It's more like "Why didn't you make me thin with clear skin and hair that doesn't always look like I combed it with a blender?"

Now, for some of you, that might not be so hard right now.

- Maybe it hasn't occurred to you to think much about beauty matters yet, like the mini-woman blogger who wrote, *"I don't worry about my appearance because I'm growing up with two older brothers and have mostly boys for friends. They don't care about all that so I don't either."*

- Maybe you've been able to totally accept that, as a tween girl said to me in an e-mail: *"Looks don't matter because it will all go away when we go to Heaven."*

- Maybe you *do* have everything it takes to be the next supermodel, so beauty isn't a problem for you.

Still, most girls between the ages of eight and twelve start thinking about the way they look at some point, and very few are completely happy with what they see when they check out their reflection in a store window. And yet it can also be (a) fun and (b) a big part of your growing closer to God. Really.

You can choose to go on an adventure that includes discovering the true, absolute, no-denying-it beauty that every girl has—that you have—instead of spending a lifetime visiting the mirror where you can always find something wrong.

> 66 Do I worry about the way I look? YES!!! I worry about stuff like whether or not my hair is perfect, that I can't wear makeup, how many pimples I have, whether or not I'm too fat. I'm really popular at my school, and I feel the need to look good. 99

So what do you say we get started?

That Is SO Me!

Before you begin the adventure part of our journey together, it's good to know where you're starting from—somewhere between "What's a mirror?" and "I want to put a bag over my head!"—and that's what this "quiz" is for. You can do it alone or with a friend you totally trust (someone with BFF status). If you're afraid a curious younger bro or sis will get those little hands on this book, keep track of your answers on another piece of paper and make confetti out of it later. This is your very private stuff.

Here's how it works: Put a star next to each thought

below that you've *ever* had for more than, like, two seconds. Even if you don't believe the thought, if it nags you sometimes, give it a star. There's no right or wrong. No good or bad. There's just you, and you won't learn anything about you if you aren't honest, right?

○ I'm fat.

○ I'm ugly.

○ I don't look that bad except for my _____.

○ I'm too tall (or short).

○ I have my father's _____ (nose, lips, etc.), which is not good.

○ I want to look like a star (model, singer, actress, etc.).

○ I'll never look like a star, which is depressing.

○ Some people tell me I'm pretty, but I don't believe them.

○ Some people tell me I'm not pretty, and I believe them.

○ I don't do that much to look prettier because it isn't gonna help.

○ I wish I were cuter so I'd have more friends.

○ I don't care about my appearance. I'm not the girly-girl type.

○ It drives me nuts to have to wear _____ (glasses, braces, a school uniform, etc.). They make me look lame.

Next step, count your stars and put your number here:

_____

Ready to score?

Got between 11 and 13 stars? This section is SO for you. You seem to be having a tough time seeing your own beauty. The adventure-journey is going to be especially amazing for you because every discovery will be a surprise. You're going to love the real you.

If you have between 4 and 10 stars, you're not alone. Most girls your age go back and forth between thinking they're not so bad and deciding they're total freaks. But read on and get a true picture of yourself that gets better all the time.

As for 0 to 3 stars, you're in a great place to have some fun with your beauty right from the start. As you read, be aware of the things you did star because we're going to chase those thoughts away.

Whatever your score, you're about to set out on an expedition. You won't turn into a model (unless that's what God has in mind for you). You won't suddenly become like the "cool" girls. But you will find your *own* cool—the beautiful person you were made to be.

> Sometimes I worry about how I look and sometimes I couldn't care less. When I'm going out to eat, I think about my outfit. But when I don't care what I look like—like when I'm going over to my friend's house—it's just because nobody else is going to care either!

> I don't want to lie here: I really do worry about my appearance. Every day I look at all the other skinny girls and I think to myself, *Why can't I be the same?*

HERE'S THE DEAL ABOUT BEAUTY

There are several things we need to agree on before we continue. We can think of them as the beauty truths we have to know and believe so that we can actually make progress.

Beauty Truth #1: Nobody is perfect. Girls in magazines and music videos might **look** perfect, but if you met one of them outside the studio, you'd see right away that she has flaws just like everybody else: a piece of hair that won't stay out of her eye, the retainer she just popped in, maybe even a zit. You don't see those things in an ad or on the movie screen because …

- a team of makeup artists, personal trainers, and wardrobe consultants were all over her before she went before the camera.

- film editors can do amazing things with digital enhancing, just the way you can in Photoshop. A couple of clicks and that piece of flyaway hair or that enormous pimple disappears.

Beauty Truth #2: It isn't healthy for you to try to look like a model right now. If you take a close look at one, you'll probably see that she doesn't have an ounce of fat on her body. Before you consider yourself a hippo because at ten years old you weigh more than she does at twenty, remember this:

- A girl who becomes a model tends to be naturally thin and very tall to begin with.

- Then it becomes part of her job to keep her weight low so the curves of her body don't take attention away from the clothes she's modeling.

- Many models diet constantly, practically living on water and celery, and they work out daily for hours on end.

Don't even think about doing that. You have healthy growing to do.

Beauty Truth #3: Boys are not to be listened to when it comes to how you look. Even if you don't care what boys think, they can mess with your image of yourself by the stuff they blurt out, so keep these things in mind:

- They're dealing with their own growing-up issues right now, so a lot of them think they have to be funny all the time so it won't show that your blossoming beauty is confusing them.

- What boys consider funny is different from what cracks you and your friends up. They think it's hilarious to call you Tinsel Teeth because you just got braces or to swat at imaginary cooties when you stand next to them. Even though you know they're just being absurd little creeps, it's normal for you to get your feelings hurt.

- Give them a few years. They'll get nicer. Meanwhile, don't take beauty tips from them.

Beauty Truth #4: Comparing yourself to the "cool" girls will get you nowhere on this journey to the beautiful you. Sometime in elementary school, it starts to become obvious that some girls are considered "cooler" than others. We don't know who decides that. Unfortunately, it just happens. Because the "cool girls" get a lot of attention and have a bunch of friends, almost everybody wants to be like them. Here's what you *don't* want to do (because it will stop you dead in your beauty tracks):

- Try to change yourself to be more like the cool girl.

- Dislike the cool girl because seeing her makes you feel so bad about yourself.

- Work overtime trying to *stay* cool (if you happen to *be* a cool girl).

None of that is any fun. And none of it makes you beautiful. It makes you stressed-out, unhappy, and resentful— but not beautiful.

Beauty Truth #5: The most beautiful women are beautiful because you like them. Think about all the girls and women you love. Don't you think these people are just so attractive?

- your best friend

- your favorite female teacher

- your cool aunt

- the cousin you want to be like

- your mom

Maybe they wouldn't be cast in the role of Cinderella, but do you know more exquisite women than they are? More than likely they feel the same way about you. Ask any one of them if she thinks you're a beautiful person, and you'll hear, "Absolutely, I do!"

Beauty Truth #6: You are already beautiful. Now, maybe …

- On the outside, you haven't "grown into yourself" yet.

- You haven't learned to make the most of what you have.

- You have hard stuff going on in your life that keeps you from really showing your beauty.

You were made to be a gorgeous human being. She's in there. How do I know that's true? I have it on the best Authority. After all, God doesn't make ugly. Okay, so maybe roaches are ugly … but the boy roaches think they're kinda cute.

Who, ME?

Name the most beautiful woman you know personally.

_____

> Every time I think I'm ugly, I feel bad because I feel like I'm insulting God's work.

> I try to be content with the way God made me, but I struggle with worrying if I'm overweight. (Especially my belly. Sheesh.)

> I have always felt big for my age because everyone around me is pretty tiny. I also get zits a lot, and that doesn't help. It feels awful to feel obsessive about my looks, so I try to think more what God is seeing and just go for it every day.

> While the inside is definitely more important than the outside, I think we should still try to look our best. Our bodies are God's temples, and God always had His temples decorated. But we have to make sure how we look isn't as important to us as what we do.

GOT GOD?

David in the Bible is a guy we trust because he was
a man after God's own heart, right? He wasn't perfect
either; he was just very close to God, close enough to
know these things that he shares in Psalm 139 (which
you might want to check out right now).

- God knows everything about you (verses 1–4).

- God is everywhere (verses 5–12).

- God created your "inmost being" (verse 13).

So, believing that all of that is true, you pretty much
have to believe that *this* is true too:

- "I praise you because I am fearfully and wonderfully
  made; your works are wonderful, I know that full
  well" (verse 14).

Fearfully, by the way, doesn't mean like Frankenstein's
monster (although even he turned out to have a soft spot).
It means **awesomely**. You were made to be awesome and
wonderful. There it is, right in the Bible. God knit you
together with love in every stitch. He thought of you, and
you **became**.

And check out verse 17:

"How precious to me are your thoughts, God!"

You are the result of God's precious thought. How cool is that! Not ...

- some modeling agency's thought (though there's nothing wrong with being a model),

- or a cool girl's thought (although a lot of cool girls are really nice),

- or that boy's thought (which he doesn't even understand himself!).

God's Thought: You are a beautiful person. Believe it. Your job on this adventure we're about to begin is to let God's "precious thought" out where it can shine like a light. Be every bit the beauty God created you to be so other people will see Christ in you and be drawn to you. Then when you love them, you show them who God is, and they're beautiful too. Ya gotta love how that works.

Okay ... go ahead and ask it ... you know you want to: *"But aren't some girls more precious than others? Don't some just naturally shine brighter?"*

Okay, picture God creating a new baby girl. Imagine the God whose works are wonderful saying, "Oops, I didn't make little Megan as precious as baby Brittany. I hate it when that happens."

Can you honestly imagine God saying that?

Uh, no. Every tiny being God creates has his beautiful fingerprints on her. She's shaped with love and "breathed through" with her own gifts and special brightness. Each child is an original. Each one is God's art. Each is priceless.

That includes you, Precious Thought. You are fearfully and wonderfully made. Your part is to uncover the beauty—inside and out. It's a journey. You ready?

● ●

YOU CAN DO IT

At the end of every chapter in this section, you'll have a chance to get your hands on all the things we've just talked about, just as you did in "Body Talk." Sometimes it'll be fun to do these activities with your BFF or a bunch of friends. This first one, though, you'll want to do alone. (Otherwise, the giggle meter will go out of control!)

What you'll need:

○ a binder with paper, or a spiral notebook, or a book you make yourself with covers and paper (but make it so you can add more pages later)

○ your fave things to write/create with (colored pencils, markers, gel pens, crayons, whatever)

○ mirror (a full-length one is best, but if you don't have one, use the biggest you can find.)

○ about thirty minutes of privacy (which is hard in some households, but give it your best shot!)

What you're doing:

You're creating a sort of travel journal for this beauty adventure you're embarking on. You can call it anything. These are just some suggestions:

○ Journey to the Beautiful Me

○ Destination: Gorgeous

○ Adventures in Beauty

○ Discovery Log

At the end of each chapter, you'll have a chance to add another page or two. Feel free to do whatever you want to set up and decorate your pages—everything from stickers and ink stamps to just plain pencil. What you come up with will be uniquely you, even though the things you'll be thinking about will be the same for every mini-woman.

This first page is called "Beauty Search."

How to make it happen:

1. On the first page of your travel journal, draw an outline of yourself, head to toe. It can be realistic or just kind of a gingerbread man shape. Keep it beside you as you go on to the next step.

2. Stand in front of the mirror and take a good long look at yourself. If put-down thoughts like "I am hideous!" or "I hate my lips!" come to mind, order them to leave the room because they aren't welcome here.

3. Look for every detail that is beautiful in your reflection. Don't say, "I don't *see* anything beautiful," because that's a big fat lie. Notice things like your nice hairline; that cute little chicken pox scar that gives your face character; your big white, shiny teeth. Check out your hair, mouth, complexion, face shape,

eyebrows, smile, eyes, chin, nose, arms, legs, height, shoulders, and hands. It's all good.

4. Write a word of description next to each part of you on the outline you drew on your page. (For example, "sparkly" could go where your eyes are. "long and slender" might go at your fingers.) Be sure everything you include is a compliment. This isn't being conceited. You're just noticing God's fine work!

5. If you have a lot of empty space on your page, look in that mirror again and add more positive things you see. Use colors if you want. You can even draw your features in. By the time you're through, you should have a page full of words that add up to a very attractive mini-woman.

6. Then grin into the mirror, because this is only the start of more great things to come.

That's What I'm Talkin' About

Here's your chance once again to journal or draw or simply think about how all the stuff you've just read applies to you. You can either fill in your answers here or write/draw them on another page of your travel journal.

Here are this chapter's things to ponder when it's just you and God talkin':

About this whole "liking what you see when you look in the mirror thing"—I think _____

_____

_____.

I never realized before that I have such nice _____

_____.

It's going to be hard for me not to keep hating my _____

_____.

After reading this chapter, I already want to _____

_____.

My question for God about my appearance is _____

_____

_____ ?

12

The Skin You're In

When I asked your fellow mini-women to share their most embarrassing beauty moments, one girl posted this comment:

> I was visiting my cousin who is eight, and I had a LOT of pimples on my forehead. They were all red and sorta bloody and gross, so I was self-conscious about them anyway. And then he just HAD to point at them in front of everyone there (the whole family) and go, 'Do you have a rash on your forehead?' and then everybody—EVERYBODY—leaned over to try to get a good view of my breakout. Talk about embarrassing!

Just So You Know

The health and beauty editor at *Girls' Life* magazine reports that 80 percent of tween girls deal with acne.

Even if your face isn't breaking out so much that an entire family reunion leans in for a closer look, taking care of your skin is still a pretty huge thing, because ...

- Your skin is the biggest organ your body has. (Crazy, huh?)

- It protects you from, well, everything.

- It regulates your body temperature.

- It holds all the inner stuff in. (Who wants her organs falling out, right?)

If your skin isn't healthy, you can't be at your best, inside or out. And, of course, if it's covered with pimples, no matter what anybody says, it's tough to *feel* like a beautiful you even though you *are*. Besides that, big breakouts aren't the only skin issues that can come up during your tween years. There's the whole tanning thing, sunburns, warts, moles, and that lovely (not!) oily shine that comes with growing from a baby girlfriend into an almost-teenager.

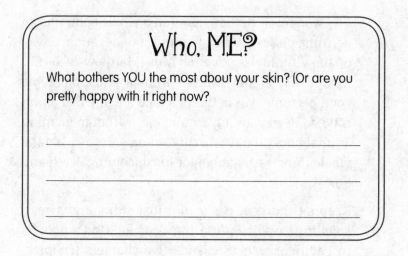

Who, ME?

What bothers YOU the most about your skin? (Or are you pretty happy with it right now?)

_____

_____

_____

Yeah, could God make it a little harder?

Actually, let's see what God really does say about skin.

● ●

GOT GOD?

Weird as it may seem, God apparently does care about our skin. Not only are there all kinds of examples of skin care in the Bible, but also it's often used as an actual *symbol* for God's love.

- Oil, which is one of the fruits of God's work (came from olives in those days), makes a person's face shine (Psalm 104:15). You aren't going to want to rub olive oil on your face at this point in your life (yikes! you make enough "grease" of your own, right?), but for those desert-dwelling people, oil was a Godsend (literally) for dry skin.

- The woman in Bethany poured a whole container of perfume on Jesus's head as an act of devotion, a way of showing lavish love for him (Matthew 26:6–13). Again, that sounds kind of strange to us, but some good perfume was actually a nice touch when a person had been walking around in dirt (not to mention animal poo) all day wearing sandals. Jesus used the whole thing as a symbol for his upcoming death and burial.

- Keeping the skin clean (not just shiny and sweet-smelling) was *really* a big deal for God's people. In Leviticus, Moses spends five chapters (chapters 11–15) giving instructions for keeping clean! Five *chapters*!

- They were still at it in Jesus' time. The Pharisees— in fact, all the Jewish people—didn't eat unless they gave their hands a ceremonial washing (Mark 7:3–4). It was part of an old tradition that was as much about being clean on the inside as on the outside.

- And when someone actually had a close encounter with God, the person's face (skin) literally shone like the sun. That happened to Moses (Exodus 34:29–30) and to Jesus (Matthew 17:2). It can even happen to you. When you truly believe in God's love, as Jesus showed it to us, even the pimpliest skin takes on a "glow."

Who, ME?

If YOU were going to pray about your skin, what would you say?

_____

_____

I'm thinking that if God pays that much attention to our skin, we pretty much need to as well. Let's start with a survey to see what kind of skin you are in.

That Is SO Me!

Your skin is as one-of-a-kind as everything else about you, but you do belong to a skin **type.** If you know what that is, you can take one-of-a-kind care of it.

This is a way different kind of "quiz" because you don't have to think about answers. You'll just need to take it on a morning when you have a little bit of extra time. Here's all you do:

1. Tear a Kleenex into four small pieces.

2. Before you wash your face, stick one piece on your forehead, one on a cheek, one on the side of your nose, and one on your chin.

3. Keep the tissue on your face for about a minute.

4. Then follow the arrows on the chart on page 257 to

see what skin type you have and what kinds of products you'll need to take care of it. When it comes to skin, one size definitely doesn't fit all.

For example, let's say the tissue doesn't even stick to your skin. Following the arrows on the chart, you'll see that you have dry skin and should look on the labels of skin cleansers for something that contains "light emollients" but no alcohol. A moisturizer that says "light" on the label is also right for you.

If the tissue sticks but doesn't look greasy, you have normal skin and should use a water-based cleanser with no alcohol and an oil-free moisturizer.

If the tissue sticks and now looks oily, you have, of course, oily skin and you'll want to use an oil-free cleanser and an oil-absorbing moisturizer, both of which can contain alcohol.

See how that works? It will make those shelves and shelves of skin products in the drugstore seem less overwhelming.

Just So You Know

If your skin gets red patches that look like a rash when you use skin-care products, you probably have sensitive skin. You'll want to use products that are labeled "For Sensitive Skin," or you can just avoid those that have fragrance in them. Whatever you use, be extra gentle with your skin. Don't scrub hard!

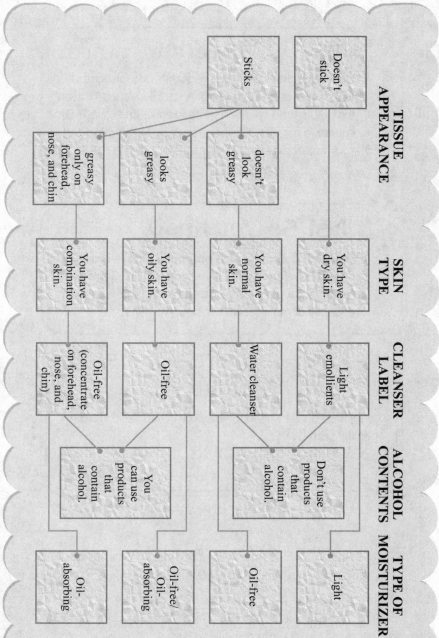

TISSUE APPEARANCE	SKIN TYPE	CLEANSER LABEL	ALCOHOL CONTENTS	TYPE OF MOISTURIZER
Doesn't stick	You have dry skin.	Light emollients	Don't use products that contain alcohol.	Light
Sticks → doesn't look greasy	You have normal skin.	Water cleanser		Oil-free
Sticks → looks greasy	You have oily skin.	Oil-free	You can use products that contain alcohol.	Oil-free/Oil-absorbing
Sticks → greasy only on forehead, nose, and chin	You have combination skin.	Oil-free (concentrate on forehead, nose, and chin)		Oil-absorbing

Just So You Know

Until about the last fifteen years, TV ads for acne treatments referred to pimples as "blemishes." Doesn't that just sound so much more ladylike than "zits"? Of course, a big ol' white-headed thing in the middle of your face feels heinous no matter what you call it.

Just So You Know

The kind of sun damage that causes cancer usually happens before a girl is twenty years old. Getting two major sunburns before age eighteen doubles your chances of getting skin cancer in your life.

Who, ME?

What food do YOU need to eat more of (or at all!) to have healthy skin?

_____

66 It'll seem like I'm just getting rid of my pimples, and then the next day they'll totally come back up. I try to keep my face clean and not wear makeup and not touch my face, like when I'm doing schoolwork. 99

> **I've got this pimple right in the folds of my mouth, and it's so hard to get products there! It's annoying and itchy!**

HERE'S THE DEAL ABOUT SKIN CARE

When I asked the mini-women on my blog what issues they had with their skin, my inbox filled up really fast! What one girl said sums up the way many of them—and maybe you—feel:

> **I do not really take care of my skin besides putting Stridex pads on it. Rarely do really big pimples come, but my nose is always covered with little ones. I look like a pepperoni pizza. I would love to have some tips on taking care of my skin.**

So let's start with some **stuff you totally need to know**, no matter what your skin type is or how closely you resemble a "pepperoni pizza."

- Wash your face morning and night—and any other time you've worked up a sweat—with a gentle soap that contains NO acids. Cleanse lightly; don't rub. Rinse with at least fifteen splashes of warm water. Your skin won't shine if it still has soap on it. Some say that to block dirt, you should make the last few splashes cold water.

- If you wear any makeup at all, always, always, always take it off before you go to bed. Otherwise, it can totally clog those pores.

- After you wash your face, smile. If your skin feels tight, put on a water-based liquid moisturizer that contains sunscreen. (We'll talk more about that later.) If your skin's really oily (you'll find that out later too), use an oil-control lotion instead of moisturizer. That should have sunscreen in it as well.

- Don't forget the rest of your skin. Take regular showers or baths and wash with gentle soap, using a loofah or a washcloth so you can get rid of dead skin cells that naturally hang out. (There are some adorable loofahs out there—decorated as everything from frogs to rock stars!) Pay attention to the following areas:

  ○ neck (Dirt can gather in the little folds.)

  ○ arms (especially those arm pits.)

  ○ elbows (A lot of people get really dark elbows, which are definitely not attractive.)

  ○ buns (Pimples love to break out there.)

  ○ legs (Knees can get smudgy, especially if you're really active.)

  ○ feet (Obviously! But be sure to get in between toes where fungus likes to grow.)

- Rinse big-time.

- When you get out of the shower or tub, use body lotion all over. You'll smell great and feel smooth. If that sounds like too much trouble, put some baby oil in a plastic spray bottle and squirt it on yourself while you're still wet. Then pat yourself dry with a towel. (Don't rub, or it will all come off.)

That might sound like a lot to remember, but if you make your skin-care routine as automatic as brushing your teeth (and I **know** you're doing that regularly ...), it'll be easy.

Another mini-woman had this to say about her skin:

> 66 I get sunburned so easy. It's like I walk out my back door, and I turn red and then later peel. I just want a tan! 99

By now, just about everyone is aware that suntans (and, of course, sun*burns*) are as bad for your skin as smoking cigarettes is for your lungs, but when you see a picture of a bronze beauty in a white swimsuit (blonde hair blowing in the ocean breeze), it's hard not to think, *I want to look like that!* Here's some **more stuff you totally need to know** that will hopefully change your mind.

The sun's rays are great for giving you vitamins and keeping you in a good mood, but they aren't so great for your skin. No matter what anybody tells you, **a tan (and certainly a sunburn) is not healthy**. It means you've damaged your skin.

The time to start protecting yourself is NOW. Here's what to do:

- When you're out in the sun soaking up vitamins between the hours of 10:00 a.m. and 4:00 p.m., wear sunscreen with an SPF (sun protection factor) of at least 15—higher if you have really fair skin—even if it's a cloudy day.

- Read the label to be sure it's no more than a year old—its effects do expire—and that it protects from both UVA and UBA rays.

- Use it on every part of your body that's exposed, including your hands. Yeah, that'll take a few minutes, but the beach isn't going anywhere.

- Reapply sunscreen every two to three hours and after you've been in the water. If you have trouble remembering to do that when you're out there having a blast in the sand and surf, ask someone to remind you (and then don't argue with her when she does!).

- Use SPF 15 lip balm on your lips too, since that thin skin burns easily.

Here's another question from a tween girl that I hear a lot:

> 66 Some people tell me that chocolate causes pimples, or like if you eat too many French fries you'll get acne. I hope that's not true because being twelve is hard enough without giving up all the stuff I like to eat! 99

There is no so-called "hard science" to prove that chocolate, greasy foods, or soft drinks actually **cause** skin breakouts (more on that later), but eating a healthy diet **does** help. You don't have to become a total health nut. Just do this:

- Make sure you get veggies, fruits, whole grains, lean protein (like chicken and fish), and some dairy products every day.

- Treats are fine now and then, but don't overdo it; savor something small and exquisite rather than devouring an entire bag of chips in front of the TV.

In case that doesn't make sense to you (like, what does food have to do with skin?), consider this: Good food has nutrients that repair skin when it gets damaged, which is constantly happening in tiny ways. Your skin has to be healthy to be pretty. Sodas and candy bars will not make you pretty. Believe it or not, broccoli will!

And here is **even more stuff you totally need to know:**

- Drink water, like between four and eight 8-ounce glasses a day. If that's hard to do when you're in school, try to grab a couple of swallows every time you pass the water fountain to flush out the icky stuff you take in just by breathing.

- Get the kind of exercise that makes you sweat, so that your skin is naturally cleansed. Doing some activity that you really dig for twenty minutes a day will perk your skin—and you—right up. So come on … off the couch! Walk the dog, get a game of screaming hide-and-seek going with your friends, practice all the cheers you know—whatever gets a smile on your face and a flush in your cheeks.

- Get at least eight to ten hours of sleep every night. While you're getting your ZZZZs, your body is busy restoring itself after everything it's been through all day, and that means your skin too.

Okay, that's the deal for everybody, even grown-ups. But what about the Plague of Puberty: **the whole pimple thing**? As one mini-woman put it in an e-mail to me:

> I have a lot of pimples, and it is awful! They show up right after I wash my face in the morning and are like, 'Ha ha, we win! Better luck next time!'

Let's look at the questions girls like you ask, and the answers that might help you.

Q Where do pimples even come from?

A The closer you get to being a teenager, the more oil your body produces. In some girls, the oil glands really get going, and that can cause clogs of dead cells and oil that get infected. Presto—pimples.

Q So, really, foods like French fries and chocolate don't cause zits?

A Nah. It's oil on the inside that makes skin break out. It may be, though, that white flour and sugar can make pimple problems worse,

so healthy eating habits are always a good
idea.

Q So how do I keep from getting pimples?

A The bad news is, sometimes you're going to
get a pimple no matter what you do. Some
people are more likely to get them because of
the amount of oil they just naturally produce.
That's a bummer, but you can prevent some
breakouts by following the skin-care routine
we've talked about.

**Q If I get one of those evil ones that's all white and
gross-looking, should I pop it?**

A No! Sit on your hands if you have to, but don't
touch that zit. If you pop it or even pick at
it, you'll spread the bacteria that has caused
the infection, and more pimples just like that
one are guaranteed to show up. The more you
touch it, the longer it will take for it to heal.
Besides, you could end up with a scar that'll be
there forever. The pimple itself will go away—
even though the rest of the day may seem like
forever.

Q Then what CAN I do? It's ugly!

A There are several things you can try on a
pimple with a white head:

○ Dab some tea tree oil on the spot with a cotton swab.

○ Before you go to bed, put hot (not boiling!)

water on the corner of a cloth and press it very gently on the pimple. Be patient, and it will open up and drain itself.

○ The next day, cover it up with a dab of a concealer if your mom has some.

Q What about those black plugs of dirt that get in my pores?

A Ah, yes, blackheads. They aren't dirt; they're skin pigment. They're created when oil and dead cells clog up a pore. They aren't infected yet, so those you can "operate on."

○ After a hot shower, squeeze VERY gently with a finger on each side of the blackhead.

○ Don't dig in with your fingernails, of course.

○ If it doesn't pop out right away, leave it alone until the next time you take a shower.

○ If you get a lot of blackheads, use a facial scrub when you wash. Rub it in with a washcloth or loofah. Be sure to be sweet with your skin while you're doing it. The grains in the scrub will do the work so you don't have to scour your face like you're cleaning a pot.

Q You're talking about a pimple or two. My face looks like I have big ol' boils. It even hurts. What do I do?

A That's the actual condition called **acne**, and it is a skin disease (though it's not catching). Here's what we know about this frustrating condition.

○ The cause is complicated, but it has to do with hormones that are produced in the teen years that tell your body to produce more oil. In some people—and we don't know why—the oil gets stuck in the glands and plugs them up. The result is a face (and sometimes chest and back) full of cysts, blackheads, and pimples.

○ Many times even after acne clears up, it leaves scars.

○ Acne usually requires special care by a skin doctor (a dermatologist). No matter how beautiful you know you are on the inside, it's hard to feel pretty when your skin is sick.

○ A dermatologist will tell you how to take care of your special skin and will probably prescribe medication in lotion and pill form to clear things up. You'll feel so much better.

○ If your mom says you'll just grow out of your acne, please show her this book. You shouldn't have to suffer the pain.

Okay, so what about **makeup**? Here's a totally true story from one of your fellow tweens that'll get us started on that subject!

66 When I was ten, everybody was wearing makeup.

Except me. I wanted to try it too, but I had NO CLUE how to do it. Recipe for disaster.

"I snuck into my mom's bag and took it into the bathroom. I had no idea what was what, so basically I put what I THOUGHT was supposed to go on top of your eyes, which I now know was eye shadow. It was BLACK, and I put it all AROUND my eyes. Then I draped my hair over one eye and posed for myself and smiled. I thought it looked cool. I added more stuff and then, powdery cheeks, lipstick, black eye and all, I confidently marched out of the bathroom, proud of my new look that I was sure everyone would fall in love with.

"But they didn't react how I thought they would. Everyone was like, 'Are you all right!? Did somebody hit you?' I said, 'Hello, anyone ever heard of MAKEUP?' My mom made me go wash it off, and that was pretty embarrassing.

"As if that wasn't ENOUGH ... it didn't exactly wash off that well and the next day I went to school with hair drooped over one eye and the remainder of what I couldn't get off of the 'shiner.' Everybody called me Emo. Obviously I haven't done THAT since!"

Maybe you've had a most embarrassing beauty moment like that. Or it could be that you haven't thought about makeup at all yet. Or you may already be telling your mom that everybody else in your class is wearing it, so why can't you? Wherever you are with the idea of blush and lip gloss and eye shadow, answers to the cosmetics questions will help you be your most beautiful you at this point in your life.

When should I start wearing makeup? Some girls are lingering over the lipstick displays at age eight, while others can't see the point of it even when they're teenagers. So, in general …

- If you're younger than twelve, it's better, for the sake of your still-delicate skin, to wait a while before putting on makeup for real. (Though you can sure have fun playing around with it. More on that later!)

- At around twelve, if you're dying to use makeup, talk (calmly!) to your parents about it. They have the final word. (So no sneaking on eye shadow in the girls' bathroom if their final word is "not yet.")

Why do you say under twelve is too early for makeup? I'm dyin' here! I've talked to a lot of parents, and here are the reasons they've come up with that actually make sense to me too.

- Makeup can make you look older than you are, and it can make you feel grown-up. But if you *aren't* older and you *aren't* grown-up, then you're not being your true self, are you?

- Being real is the best beauty treatment of all.

- And walking around with a scowl on your face because your dad says no to makeup will NOT be a good look for you.

I'm allowed to wear some makeup, but I don't know how much is okay. If you and your parents agree that a little makeup would be all right, you'll still want to be "the best you at your age." You aren't trying to cover anything up or create something that isn't there, so your best look will be ...

- sheer lip colors and glosses

- a little natural-looking mascara

- some blush that's the color your skin turns when you exercise.

That will bring out your natural beauty, and that's what makeup is always supposed to do.

How do I know how to put it on? It looks so complicated! Yeah, before you wear makeup outside your house, you definitely need to have someone show you how to apply it. Just don't ask somebody who seems to put on her own makeup with a putty knife—or without a mirror!

I like the idea of wearing makeup and my parents say I can, but I don't think I want to wear it all the time. So when do I?

- You might want to start with some pretty lip gloss on special occasions.

- Maybe from there you could wear it on the weekends, when you and your friends are getting together, that kind of thing.

- Whether you break out the lip color and blush for school depends on school rules, your parents' guidelines, and how much attention you want to pay to your mirror when you have stuff to do.

What if I REALLY want to wear makeup and my parents won't let me? Obviously, they have the last word, but there are fun things you can do to feel more polished without breaking the rules.

- Use lip balm, which not only keeps your lips healthy, but also makes them feel like you have lipstick on.

- Put some petroleum jelly on the tips of your eyelashes to make them look darker and longer (just don't get it in your eyes).

- While you're waiting for the day to come when you'll have a whole collection of shadows and blushes and other fun things in your makeup case, take great care of your skin, be your best self, and remember that you are already beautiful. Let makeup just be something fun to look forward to.

> I have TONSSSSS of PIMPLES!!!!! But besides that, I guess I do think my skin is beautiful. It's really smooth, and it's a color tone that's not too pale and not too tan. It's never gotten sunburned, and it's really soft. The only problem with it is the breakouts, so my mom's going to take me to a dermatologist.

> Just because I have acne doesn't make me think I'm not beautiful.

Who, ME?

What was YOUR most embarrassing beauty moment?

_____

_____

Just So You Know

Research done with 250 girls at the AllyKatzz Tween Girl Summit showed that tweens don't WANT to use makeup, but they live in a culture that tells them they need improvement.

YOU CAN DO IT

Discovering your most beautiful self is supposed to be fun, not just another THING ya gotta do, like chores and homework! So let's make some fun. **Makeup Madness** is a time to play around with makeup, purely for giggles, even if wearing it in public is years away for you. The **Skin Spa** will get you glowing and feeling like your prettiest self. At the end, we'll add another page or two to your travel journal.

You can do this with a BFF or two (or even your mom). Just set up a place where you won't be interrupted by teasing brothers, curious fathers, etc. Your mom's bedroom and bathroom are ideal, but even the kitchen will work. Make it as special as you want with candles, flowers, pretty towels, and favorite music.

What you'll need for Makeup Madness:

○ all the makeup you and your buds can gather that can be put on with fingers or cotton swabs (eye shadow applicators, mascara brushes, and eyeliner used by other people carry bacteria you don't need to share; lipstick is the exception, since it can be wiped off with a tissue)

○ mirrors, especially the ones on stands, or just one big bathroom mirror if there's room for everybody at the counter

○ lots of tissues, washcloths (dark colors are best), cotton swabs, and towels

○ hair thingies (for getting hair out of faces)

○ magazines with pix of girls in cool (or even bizarre!) makeup

What you're doing:

You're going to do makeovers on each other, whether "for real" or just to see how many different "yous" you can create, just for fun. You'll have a blast, and you'll also see that the natural you is probably the prettiest after all.

How to make it happen:

1. Lay down some limits. (No clown faces, no going nuts and trashing your mom's bathroom, etc.) Since makeup is a grown-up thing, you'll want to act accordingly, yes?

2. Then anything goes as you try on different looks, some original, some copying the mags. Experiment with techniques. Go glam, then country girl cute, then on-stage—anything you want.

3. Laugh.

4. Tell each other you're gorgeous.

5. Take pictures.

When you've had as much fun as you can stand, it's time to wash it off, so do that big-time first, and then move on to the Skin Spa.

What you'll need for the Skin Spa:

○ 1 cup of uncooked oats

○ ½ cup of plain yogurt

○ 2 tablespoons of honey

○ mashed bananas or strawberries (optional)

What you're doing:

You're mixing a facial mask that will make your skin as smooth and soft as a baby's. And in the process, you are going to **laugh** at each other, guaranteed, because everybody (even that **Seventeen** model) looks hilarious in this getup.

How to make it happen:

It's SO easy …

1. Put all the ingredients in a blender, and puree it until

you have a rough cream. If you're adding fruit, use bananas for dry skin, strawberries for normal; skip the fruit if your skin is super oily.

2. Spread the mixture on your face with your fingers in an even layer, and let it dry for five minutes. (This is the time when the giggle meter goes nuts.)

3. Wash the mask off with warm water, and pat dry with a clean towel.

4. Stroke your face to feel how soft and smooth it is. Beautiful.

5. Store the leftover mixture in an air-tight container in the fridge for up to two weeks.

6. You can repeat this once a day, but no more than that. See if you can do it once a week.

You'll be feeling pretty gorgeous by then. Time to snuggle in with a healthy snack and maybe your all-time fave BFF movie.

When you're alone again, you can add another page to your travel journal (whatever you're calling it from chapter 11). Create a new page called "The Skin I'm In." Copy these headings onto the page, and fill them in. Be as artsy as you want, of course—colored ink, drawings, even photos from your Make-Up Madness and Skin Spa party.

- **My Skin Type**

- **Products to Use**

- **Things to Try for Pimples**

- **Other Stuff I Need to Start Doing**

That's What I'm Talkin' About

Just as you did at the end of chapter 11, journal or draw or simply think about how all the stuff you've just read applies to you. You can either fill in your answers here, or write/draw them on another page of your travel journal.

Here are this chapter's things to ponder when it's just you and God talkin':

The best thing about the skin God gave me is _____

_____.

The biggest change I'm going to make in taking care of my skin is _____

_____.

The way I feel about makeup is _____

_____.

When it comes to my skin, I really need to talk to my mom about _____

_____.

My question for God about my skin is _____

_____

_____?

13

Love the 'Do

You would think mini-womanhood would be a time of ponytails and French braids and cute bobs and fun bows. Maybe *sometimes* it is, but according to the tween girls I talk to, hair can be just as much about the frizzies, the greasy swoop, and tangles that look like a rodent has taken up residence on your head. Here's what one of your fellow tweens wrote in a comment:

> I hate my hair. It used to be naturally almost white blonde until I turned eleven, and now it's dirty blonde with hidden lighter streaks in it in random places. It's ridiculously frizzy when I get out of the shower, and it stays that way unless I straighten it. It also gets super

greasy if it isn't washed about every two days. I wish everybody but me was bald. Then everybody would think I was pretty. I'm so frustrated with my hair; I told my mom I was gonna get a Mohawk this summer if a miracle doesn't happen. **"**

"I have frequent bad hair days. **"**

You're probably not thinking of doing anything quite that drastic. Maybe you're even one of those girls who wakes up in the morning with a head of hair that barely needs to be combed. More than likely you're somewhere in between, wondering how you're going to get down the find-your-own-beauty trail with your particular tresses, especially since they may not be behaving the way they used to when you were a shorter child.

Just So You Know

When you Google "tweens and hair," you get 589,000 results!

Wherever you are with hair, this chapter is here to convince you that *every* girl can have hair that's great for her. Really. Before we go there, let's talk about striking a good balance between freaking out over the hair thing and ignoring your 'do completely (until you have a monster knot on your head). God has some help for you.

> **"** I don't really care about my hairdo that much and my friends don't either ... but some kids at my school do. Yesterday these two girls came to volleyball practice with this wacky lopsided bun at the tippy-top of their head. I was like, 'Huh?' **"**

> **"** I was born with curly hair, and now I've straightened it. Is that bad? Isn't that like altering what God gave me? Because I'm starting to wonder. **"**

• •

GOT GOD?

With all God has to do, do you think he really cares about your hair? People in the Bible sure seemed to think so.

- "Do not cut the hair at the sides of your head or clip off the edges of your beard" (Leviticus 19:27) is written as part of God's message through Moses to the entire assembly of Israel on how to be holy. Some Orthodox Jewish men still follow that rule to show total obedience to God. You'll see them with ringlets in front of their ears.

- In Numbers 6:5, God said that if a man or woman wanted to make a special vow (a period of special devotion to God), one of the requirements was to not cut the hair on the head. You'd know a God-devoted person by the long 'do.

- In the New Testament, Luke 7:44 tells about a woman who washed Jesus' feet with her tears and dried them with her hair. She also kissed his feet and poured perfume on them. Jesus was impressed by how deeply she loved him. You *would* have to love someone a lot to dry his wet feet with your own hair.

And that has what to do with you now?

For us it's more of a symbolic thing than it is instructions for washing and cutting—or not cutting! In Matthew 10:30 Jesus says, "And even the very hairs of your head are all numbered." That shows how much you're worth to God. Even if people hate you because you stand up for him, Jesus said, "Not a hair of your head will perish" (Luke 21:18).

The apostle Peter warns us women not to get so focused on our hair that we forget about being beautiful on the inside. Beauty, he writes in 1 Peter 3:4, "should be that of your inner self, the unfading beauty of a gentle and quiet spirit, which is of great worth in God's sight." (More on that in our last chapter.)

Yes, take care of every hair God counted and put on your head. Enjoy it. And match its beauty with your actions. You won't just be that girl with the pretty long brown hair. You'll be that really friendly (or nice or fun or crazy-but-I-like-her) girl with the pretty long brown hair.

> *Who cares what everybody else thinks about your hair? It's YOUR hair, and if you feel beautiful, you'll look beautiful because you'll be smiling, which makes you look incredible.*

HERE'S THE DEAL ABOUT BASIC HAIR CARE

We're going to look in a minute at how your hair is You-nique, but let's start with some things every mini-woman needs to know about hair care. In case you're one who has to be bribed into taking a shower, have no fear. These are just basics that require less time than it takes to wail, "I just washed my hair last week!"

- **Mane Thing #1**: Hair looks best when it's clean, so shampoo your hair as soon as it gets the least bit stringy. Don't wait 'til it's matted to your head, especially if your hair is becoming oily these days, which happens naturally as you grow toward teenager-hood.

- **Mane Thing #2**: Use the right kind of shampoo for your hair.

- **Mane Thing #3**: It's okay to wash your hair every day, especially if it's oily or you play sports. Since most shampoos are too strong to use every day, just get an empty shampoo bottle and fill it halfway with your shampoo and the rest of the way with warm water. Remember, you're being gentle with your beauty.

- **Mane Thing #4**: We say we're washing our hair, but we're really washing our head.

○ Put a quarter-size glob of shampoo in the palm of your hand and work it into your wet scalp.

○ Don't scratch with your fingernails, though. Use the pads of your fingers and massage.

○ Enjoy. Even if you aren't a girly girl, washing your hair can still be kind of fun. Remember when as a kid you made bunny ears with your lathered-up hair in the bathtub? Who says you can't still do that?

○ When you rinse, your hair will get the benefits of the shampoo. Unless you use a lot of product on your hair (mousse, gel, hairspray), you don't have to worry about the ends of your hair.

○ Rinse for two or three minutes. Really. If you leave shampoo in your hair, it won't shine. It's tempting to hurry to be done so you can get back to your video game or talk on the phone to your BFF, but let hair-washing time be your good alone time.

• **Mane Thing #5**: You probably don't have to use conditioner unless your hair gets really tangled when you wash it (or you use products like gel when you style).

○ A tiny dollop the size of a dime is plenty. Just apply it to the tangled places.

○ Too much conditioner can build up on your hair so it loses its shimmer.

• **Mane Thing #6**: Always comb wet hair. Brushing it can actually break it.

- If you have trouble with tangles, use a comb with really big, spread-out teeth.

- Be slow and gentle. (Getting beautiful should never be painful!)

- **Mane Thing #7**: Brush your hair before you go to bed at night (only if it's not wet, of course).

  - If you have oily hair, brushing will spread the oils around to the right places.

  - If you have dry hair, it will bring out the natural oils.

  - Even if you have "normal" hair, brushing it is great for your scalp. It's kind of a soothing thing to do while you're thinking your end-of-the-day thoughts or listening to somebody read or whatever you do before you check out for the night.

- **Mane Thing #8**: Brush or comb your hair anytime during the day when it gets out of control, like post-soccer practice or after a math test when you've been winding it around your finger while you concentrate. Just keep a small nylon-bristle brush in your backpack, give your tresses a few strokes, and you're gorgeous.

- **Mane Thing #9**: Have your hair trimmed about every six weeks. It doesn't keep making new cells like your skin does, so the ends start to look damaged if they're not cut off.

  - If your hair is long, taking off the funky ends will make it look healthier.

- If it's short, a trim will keep the style neat and fun.

- If you're trying to let it get longer, regular trims will keep it looking good. Split ends are basically dead, so they won't grow.

There you go. That's all there is to it. Doing these mane things will make your hair healthy and clean, and you're going to feel good about that. When you feel good, you look good. It just happens.

That Is SO Me!

My hair is ...

○ a. very curly, or frizzy, or both.

○ b. greasy when I skip a day of washing.

○ c. soft but not greasy.

If you checked **a**, your hair is considered dry. You'll want to use a moisturizing shampoo. If you wash your hair every day, try baby shampoo.

If you chose **b**, you have oily hair (like you hadn't picked up on that!), so get yourself a clarifying shampoo. (It'll say that on the label.)

If choice **c** describes you, you have normal hair (which doesn't make everybody else ABnormal!), so naturally you'll want shampoo that says it's for "normal hair."

“ My hair is OILY, OILY, OILY, and people say stuff like 'Girl, do you EVER wash your hair?' ”

> It is so annoying when I have to brush my hair out twice a day just to keep it from getting knotted. My advice if you have long, tangly hair like mine: braid it before you go to bed at night. It really helps.

> I think hairstyles are a part of people. They just don't define them.

That Is SO Me!

1. Go to the mirror, which hopefully is now becoming your friend.

2. Pull your hair back so you can really see the shape of your face.

3. If it's okay with your mom, trace the shape on the mirror with the corner of a bar of soap. (Just be sure to wash it off when you're done; moms appreciate that.)

4. On a piece of paper, draw the shape you see.

5. Circle the shape that comes closest to yours:

   ○ very round

   ○ oval

   ○ square or square-ish

   ○ long-rectangular

   ○ triangular

   ○ heart-shaped

6. Love that shape. It's you! It's super easy to find a hairstyle for your special face shape. See some suggestions for you in the next section.

HERE'S THE DEAL ABOUT STYLIN'

You can stop with the basics if you want to, but what if you'd like to do more than just wash your hair and get regular trims? First, you'll want to discover a style that suits your face. If you want to be like your friends who all wear ponytails every day, go for it. That's okay. If, on the other hand, you want to try out something that's really you, let's start by discovering what general shape your face takes (even though there's not another one on earth exactly like yours).

Very round—You precious thing!

- Long and straight is good.

- Or maybe a little height on top (hair tie, anyone?) with some shape at the sides (the rest of your hair covering your ears, maybe).

- If you want your face to look even rounder, go for short and curly. You get to choose.

Oval—Have at it, girl! Any style looks great on you. How fun is that?

Square or square-ish—This means your jaw and your forehead are kind of even. You can look way classy with a face like yours.

- Just keep your haircut above or below your jawline.

- Chopped off right at your jawline or poofiness going

on at the corners of your forehead won't be your very best looks.

Long-rectangular—You can really look dramatic if you want to!

- You'll look fabulous with something fun and full at the sides.
- Avoid piling your hair right at the top of your head or wearing it too long and straight.

Triangular—Great face for having some fun with bangs and different angles.

- Try a ponytail that's off center.
- Smooth hair at your jawline is spectacular on you.

Heart-shaped—You're a walking valentine!

- Curls or something else soft at your jawline is made for you.
- Try not to go poofy on top, though.

Just So You Know

If you blow-dry your hair every day (and especially if you use a curling iron, hot rollers, or a flat iron), towel dry your hair before you style with any of those. That will cut down on the time your hair is exposed to heat that can make it brittle.

That Is SO Me!

Choose the description that sounds the most like YOUR hair …

○ My hair could be in hot rollers the whole day, and the curls will be gone an hour after I take the rollers out (if not sooner).

○ If I wash my hair and just let it air dry, it's so tangled and bushy, it won't calm down.

○ My hair takes forever to dry after I wash it, and if I don't do anything with it, it gets wild.

○ I have a lot of hair, but it's so soft it just wants to lie down flat.

○ I don't have any of those issues with my hair.

HERE'S THE DEAL ABOUT THE FRIZZIES (AND OTHER BAD-HAIR-DAY CULPRITS)

Does this sound familiar?

66 Some of my friends just wake up and their hair is gorgeous. When I don't do anything with my hair, it sticks out everywhere and is really annoying. 99

66 My hair will never lay straight. It's forever staticky. 99

> **"**My biggest complaint about my hair is that it's thick and frizzy and does whatever it wants. I want it to be shiny.**"**

They're all talking about the **texture** of hair, and it's a definite factor in choosing a style that will, as one mini-woman put it, "co-operate with you."

Don't bother even trying to change the texture of your hair because it isn't going to happen. And why would you want it to? Part of the beauty journey is discovering what works and going with it. Here's how.

○ Choice A—**Straight and Soft**

  ○ **Your best approach**: Try a bob, or wear your hair long and all one length.

○ Choice B—**Curly and Maybe Frizzy**

  ○ **Your best approach**: Have your hair cut in layers, not all one length.

○ Choice C—**Thick and Coarse**

  ○ **Your best approach**: Try different lengths all together and wear it medium to long. A stylist can thin your hair with special styling shears— but not every time you get your hair cut.

○ Choice D—**Thick and Fine**

  ○ **Your best approach**: You'll look great with your hair all one length except for layers around your face.

○ Choice E—**Co-operative**

　○ **Your best approach**: Appreciate your hair!

HERE'S THE DEAL ABOUT YOUR RACE AND YOUR HAIR

Your *ethnic background* is another thing to consider when you're talking hair. It's a huge part of being true to who you are. I realized this when I read an e-mail from an African-American mini-woman:

> 66 I had really super curly hair because I'm black, but I had it straightened recently at a salon so it will be straight for like three months. I like my straight hair because it's so much easier to take care of. My advice for people with hair like mine is use Moroccan Oil because it makes your hair soft and kind of shiny and makes it healthy. If you do straighten your hair, definitely use a protection spray or it will get really damaged. 99

So, a few tips for you:

- **If you're Asian**, women all around you are probably suffering from hair envy. (They should read this book, shouldn't they?) You are exquisite with a simple, straight cut. Don't ever let anyone talk you into getting a perm!

- **If you're Latino or Hispanic**, have a blast with your thick, shiny hair. You don't have to look for complicated haircuts because you're fabulous with shoulder-length or longer hair. And don't even think about changing the color.

- **If you're African-American**, you have so many choices, like cornrows in fun patterns, or super short and easy. One of the coolest ones, if you get frustrated with your hair, is to slick it back, which shows off your wonderful face. Don't fight your hair. Be proud of your heritage.

HERE'S THE DEAL ABOUT TRYING A TOTALLY NEW HAIRSTYLE

If you're serious about going with a way-different style based on what you've just learned about your hair, these are some things to do to make sure your new look will be a success.

- Look through magazines for girls your age and find pictures of hairstyles like the ones suggested in this book for your shape and texture. Decide if you like any of them.

- After discussing it with your mom, take this book (and a picture if you found one) to the best stylist your family can afford. That can even be your aunt who makes everybody's hair look great. Your dad's barber … maybe not.

- Explain—or have whoever takes you explain—what you want and ask the stylist if it's a good choice. If you're getting a really big change and you get nervous, you can always start with a good trim, then next time go shorter.

- Don't expect to look exactly like the girl in the picture. (That's a no-brainer, right?)

- If you end up with the worst haircut on the planet— at least to you—remember that hair grows back. Get out the barrettes or headbands or clips and use this time as a chance to experiment. Wearing a hat 24/7 is not an option because if your hair is clean and you're smiling, you're still beautiful. Got that?

HERE'S THE DEAL ABOUT "SPECIAL" HAIR ISSUES

There's never a reason to stress about your tresses, but if you want to look polished and your hair just won't cooperate, try these hints.

Does your naturally curly hair get the frizzies?

- Rub a little gel between your fingers and then run your fingers through your just-washed, wet hair. Comb your hair into place, and let it air dry.

- Or if you want to blow it dry, use a **diffuser**, which is a cone-shaped thing that goes over the end of your dryer. Once you're through, keep your hands out of your hair. Every time you touch it, it gets frizzier.

- Don't go outside in humid weather with damp hair.

Is your hair baby thin?

- Use a **volumizing** shampoo. It coats your hair and makes it look thicker.

- Don't use conditioner unless your hair really tangles, and then just use the tiniest bit.

- When you blow-dry, bend over at the waist, let your hair hang down, and blast away until it's almost dry. Then stand up straight and style it into place.

Do you wish your hair was another color?

- It's fun to think about, but just let your hair be its natural color for now. Once you start coloring it, you have to keep doing it unless you want funky roots. You have enough other fun stuff to do.

- Color-treated hair requires extra care and products. Do you really want to go there right now?

- Your hair may not stay the color it is. Most blondes, for example, get darker as they get older. Wait to see how it turns out.

- Because your hair is still pretty delicate at this age, eighteen is really the earliest you should consider doing any color treating. Even then, keep in mind that it's hard to keep artificially colored hair healthy unless you have it done professionally. Then you're talking some big bucks.

Just So You Know

Hair is a bunch of dead cells that build up into strands that come out of your head (and your arms, legs, and arm pits—lovely, huh?), so it's very fragile. If you want it to be beautiful, you have to be nice to it.

YOU CAN DO IT

Hair is probably even more fun than skin to "play" with, so let's go all out on this one. "Make-Your-Own Hair Conditioner" will get your hair shiny and soft and ready for stylin'. "The Mini-Woman Salon" is a time to experiment with various 'dos, whether just for giggles or for real. At the end, we'll make another entry to your travel journal.

You can do this with a BFF or two (or even your mom). Again, just set up a place where you won't be interrupted by people who just don't get the hair thing. It's way fun to go for a salon look, with drapes to go over your clothes, all your supplies laid out on the counter, and great hairstyle pics all over the place.

What you'll need for Make-Your-Own Hair Conditioner:

○ 1 tablespoon of oil (olive oil or any vegetable oil)

○ 1 egg yolk (not the whole egg)

○ a dish that's microwave safe (and, obviously, a microwave!)

○ a whisk or fork

○ a shower cap or plastic bag just big enough to cover your head (not your face!)

○ shampoo for your hair type

What you're doing:

You're mixing a conditioner that, though it will feel weird at first (as most fun things do), will leave your hair feeling silky and looking shiny. In the process, you're going to make some pretty interesting EWWW sounds, which is why this is so much better when you do it with somebody you love to hoot and howl with.

How to make it happen:

How easy is this, really?

1. Put the oil in the microwave-safe dish, and microwave it for five seconds.

2. Add the egg yolk. (Ask your mom how to separate the egg if you don't know how.)

3. Whisk until blended, using a whisk or a fork.

4. Massage the mixture into your hair. (I *told* you it was going to feel weird!)

5. Put on a shower cap or a plastic bag. (Not over your face, obviously!)

6. Leave it on for twenty minutes. This is a great time for a snack or for reading ahead to find out what the "Mini-Woman Salon" is all about.

7. When twenty minutes are up, shampoo your hair (with your hair-type shampoo) and rinse well.

8. Enjoy your luxurious hair!

What you'll need for the Mini-Woman Salon:

○ A clean comb and brush for each person. Even though your hair has just been washed, it's better not to share "hair utensils."

○ A blow dryer.

○ Curling iron, flat iron, and hot rollers are optional (and should only be used with a grown-up's permission since you can burn yourself with them).

○ All the barrettes, headbands, bows, ribbons, hair ties, and other cool hair stuff you and your fellow stylists can gather.

○ Pictures of hairstyles you'd like to try—and plenty of imagination!

What you're doing:

You're going to experiment with hairstyles just for fun, although if you use the suggestions in this chapter, you might just discover a new 'do that's perfect for you—for real! This can be so totally fun, and that's what finding your beautiful you is all about.

How to make it happen:

1. Set some boundaries (no dyeing hair, going wild with hair spray, making people look ridiculous on purpose).

2. Just let your creativity flow as you try on different

looks, some taken from the pictures you've collected, some you make up yourself.

3. Giggle (of course).

4. Give each other lavish compliments.

You'll be feeling pretty good about your sweet self by the time you're done. You might want to finish up with your own photo shoot and, of course, a healthy snack or some small exquisite treat.

When you're alone again, you can add another page to your travel journal (whatever you're calling it, from chapter 11). Create a new page called "The Mane Thing". Copy these headings onto the page, and fill in the information. Be as creative as you want, of course—maybe using colored ink, drawings, even photos from your conditioner-making fest and your salon.

- **My Hair Type**

- **Shampoo to Use**

- **My Face Shape/Hair Texture**

- **Hair Style to Try**

That's What I'm Talkin' About

Just as you've been doing at the ends of the previous chapters, journal or draw or simply think about how all the stuff you've just read applies to you. You can either fill in your answers here or you can write/draw them on a page of your travel journal.

Here are this chapter's things to ponder when it's just you and God talkin':

The best thing about the hair God gave me is _____

_____.

The biggest change I'm going to make in taking care of my hair is _____

_____.

The way I feel about taking the time to do my hair is _____

_____.

If I could change one thing about my hair *attitude* it would be _____

_____

_____.

My question for God about the whole hair thing is _____

_____

_____ ?

14

Smooth Moves

As we mentioned in the "Body Talk" section, things get a little hairier during your tween years. Fuzz in places you never really thought about before can suddenly make just going swimming a big deal. Here's what one mini-woman told me:

> My favorite cousin and I were at the pool, and he pointed to my legs and said, 'You need to shave, Lady.' He's always been a big-time joker, and it wasn't meant to hurt. Still, I was a little embarrassed. I just said, 'You're lookin' a little furry yourself, Man Dude!' He just laughed and started showing his leg hair even more. Me, I went home later and asked my mom if I could shave my legs.

I thought she'd say yes because I was already shaving my armpits, but she said no, that if I did, it would come back stronger and darker and I'd just have to keep doing it. I WANT to keep doing it! If my cousin noticed my hairiness, other people probably do too.**"**

Just So You Know

We girls didn't start going for the smooth look until it became acceptable to show our arms and legs in public, around the 1920s. Before that, what was the point if you were all covered up with ten tons of clothing? In some countries, ladies still skip the whole shaving thing and nobody bats an eye.

If you're on the younger end of mini-womanhood— eight or nine—or you have very little body hair, or your hair is so blonde it's almost invisible, you might be tempted to skip this chapter. But sooner or later most girls at least think about smoothing things out a little. Since that can involve items like razors, it's good to have all the information you can get so you can make your decisions about shaving and plucking and waxing …

Who, ME?

Have YOU ever been teased about hairy stuff?

_____

> ❝ I don't shave, but I might have to soon. I put lotion on my legs and instead of baby soft, it's kinda spiky. ❞

> ❝ I'm almost thirteen, so when do you suggest I should shave? ❞

Before you run off in terror (razors? really?), let's just check out your furry-ness factor and then go from there.

That Is SO Me!

In EACH ROW of boxes below, check the ONE that is most like you. (You can even add your own answer if you want to. After all, every girl is unique.)

Underarm hair:

☐   ☐   ☐

Got none   Light 'n' fuzzy   Dark and thick

I get sweat on my shirt under my arms:

☐   ☐   ☐

Almost never   When I'm way active   Whenever I move! (almost)

Leg hair:

☐   ☐   ☐

Almost none   I can barely see it.   A person across the the **room** can see it.

My hair 'tude:

☐   ☐   ☐
What body   It's not a   I want it off!
hair?   big deal.

Why I want to shave:

☐   ☐   ☐
I don't!   Some of my   I feel like an ape.
                  friends do it.

Time I spend on beauty:

☐   ☐   ☐
As little as   The basics   As much as I can
possible   (almost) daily   get away with

How many boxes on the left did you check? _____

How many boxes in the center did you check? _____

How many boxes on the right did you check? _____

If you had the most checks on the left side, you probably won't want to add shaving your legs and underarms to your beauty routine yet. Read on, though, because someday you might, and as I've said, it's good to know what you're doing when you're handling a razor!

If most of your checks were in the center, you might not be up for shaving your legs yet, but it's a good idea to keep an eye on your underarms, especially if you sweat there. Hair in the pits tends to hold perspiration where it can get a little smelly. A less-than-lovely odor wafting from under your arms is definitely not beautiful. Read on and we'll show you how to take care of that and your legs when you're ready.

Were most of your checks on the right side? You may have been eyeing your dad's razor for some time, or you've recently started feeling as woolly as the family pet. That means it's the right time to approach your mom about shaving. This chapter will tell you all the secrets of hair removal, so that once she gives the okay, you're ready to de-fuzz.

66 My mom still thinks of me as seven, so I don't have the nerve to ask her anything about the tween years, and especially about shaving my legs. 99

66 I don't shave, and I don't really think I need to, but some girls in my class do and they're only like eleven. One of them is even waxing!! Ouch!! 99

GOT GOD?

You don't have to ask your mom if you can shampoo your hair or wash your face, but when it comes to shaving legs and armpits or waxing eyebrows, that's the *first* thing you need to do. The Bible doesn't have much to say about shaving. (There's that one passage in Ezekiel where God told him, "Take a sharp sword and use it as a barber's razor to shave your head and your beard" [Ezekiel 5:1], but do I even need to tell you not to attempt to shave your legs with a *sword*?) So there's nothing bad about either removing hair or not removing hair.

But God does mention the fact that if your mom says you're too young to shave your legs, and you're feeling like Tarzan, you still need to "Honor your father and your mother, *so that you may live long in the land the LORD your God is giving you*" (Exodus 20:12, emphasis added). It doesn't get much more clear than that!

So try not to let your mother's refusal to let you smooth those legs with a razor become a huge deal in your mind. Be responsible about the rest of your beauty care and revisit the issue with Mom in a few months. A little maturity goes a long way.

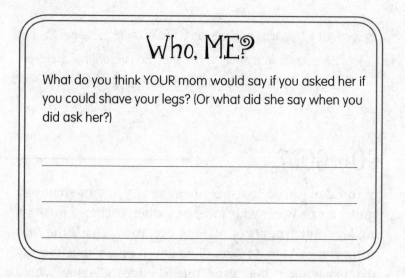

Who, ME?

What do you think YOUR mom would say if you asked her if you could shave your legs? (Or what did she say when you did ask her?)

_____

_____

_____

"I'm eleven, and I've been shaving since I was nine. I'm Italian so I'm really hairy!**"**

HERE'S THE DEAL ABOUT REMOVING LEG HAIR

> I'm twelve, and I've been shaving for a year or so. When I don't shave, the hair is really long, thick, and hard. If I skip more than a couple of days, it's actually worse than it was before.

Once you have permission to streamline your legs and/or underarms, be sure you're ready to commit to regular "defurrings" because the hair you take off, whether you use a razor, an electric shaver, or a lotion hair remover, will grow back coarser and thicker. It won't make you ugly, but you might not be happy with the prickly, stubbly look (or feel!).

> My mom says I can shave my legs, but I don't exactly know how to do it ...

All you need are these simple **shaving directions**:

1. *Gather your stuff in the shower.* This is the best place to shave because your hair will be soft. You'll need ...

   ○ Shaving cream (the thickest you can get your hands on). Ask if you can use your dad's the first time. The men's stuff is the best.

   ○ If that's not available, use hair conditioner. (Shaving dry can give you a rash.)

   ○ A razor with a clean blade. Plain disposable razors are harder to use on the bumps (like your knees), so if you do use one, try the kind with lotion built in around the blade. Throw it away after using it two or three times.

2. *With soap, wash the area you're going to shave.* Since shaving cream and hair conditioner aren't soap, they won't fight bacteria. Take care of that first.

3. *Lather up.* It's really fun to cover your legs and underarms with rich, creamy shaving lather. Besides, it helps the hair stand up so the razor can catch it.

   ○ Lather one underarm, and shave it.

   ○ Then lather and shave the other.

   ○ Then one leg, then the other.

   ○ Obviously, turn off the shower or step out of the water's stream while you're shaving, or your lather will just go down the drain.

4. *Shave.* Take your time!

   ○ Start at the top of your armpit, and—pushing down VERY GENTLY with the razor—pull it toward the bottom in short strokes. As the shaving cream comes off, so will the hair.

   ○ When shaving your legs, be sure you have steady footing on a bathmat before propping the leg you're going to shave on the side of the bathtub or the ledge.

   ○ Start at your ankle and work your way up in long, smooth strokes.

   ○ Since the hair on your thighs is finer, lighter, and shorter, you don't usually have to shave your thighs.

○ Run the razor under the water when it gets goopy with shaving cream.

5. *Be extremely careful!*

○ Go slow around bones that stick out.

○ It helps to bend your knee before shaving it.

○ Pay attention and don't rush. In fact, don't even shave if you're in a hurry.

6. (If you need first aid when you get out of the shower, you were probably going too fast. Relax. This is *YOU* time.)

○ If you do cut yourself shaving, don't freak out. It looks like you're bleeding a lot because there are more capillaries (tiny blood vessels) under your skin in the areas where you're shaving than there are in tougher places like your elbows or the bottoms of your feet. Rinse out the cut, then press it with a tissue when you get out of the shower and apply a Band-Aid.

> ❝ I thought using Nair lotion would be an easier way to get the hair off of my legs than shaving, but I ended up having an allergic reaction to it. ❞

Not everyone will break out in a rash from using a hair-removal cream or lotion, but since those products contain strong chemicals, it's a good idea to test out a little bit on a small area of your skin and wait to see how you react. Before you decide to go for it, remember that things like Nair take longer than shaving because you have to leave it on for five to ten minutes. If you plan to use it on your legs, that's going to require a lot of lotion, which gets expensive. Besides all that, it can smell funky.

If you try it, be sure to follow the package directions exactly and …

- Always wash your hands thoroughly when you're done.

- Do NOT get it in your eyes.

- Don't use it if you have even the tiniest cut or scrape.

> ❝ How do I know whether to use one of those automatic shavers or just a plain razor? ❞

You may have seen your dad shave his face (or head!) with an electric or battery-operated shaver and thought, "Wow, that looks way easier (not to mention safer!) than what I'm doing in the shower!" The only real drawback to a shaver is that unless you use a top-of-the-line one, you aren't going to get that smooth feel that a razor gives. Still, if Dad's willing to share …

> ❝ Some girls I know go with waxing instead of shaving, but … does it hurt? ❞

Actually, there are two other ways to remove leg hair, and one of them is **waxing**. Beauty salons will gladly use warm wax to remove your hair, but, yeah, it can hurt some. You have to wait two weeks before you can have it done again, which isn't all bad since the hair doesn't grow back as quickly as after you shave.

The other way is **laser hair removal**. A professional has to do that, and it definitely lasts longer than any other method. It's way expensive and takes more time than you're going to want to sit still for, I guarantee.

> When I get older, my mom is going to do a body sugaring on me. She says it's like waxing, only it's gentler and safer. I don't think I'll ever shave.

Just So You Know

Doctors say there is no problem with girls as young as eight waxing, except for the bikini area. They say save that for when you're older.

Who, ME?

Put a big ol' check mark next to the method you think YOU will use when/if you remove the hair from your legs.

    hair removal cream

    shaving

    waxing

    laser hair removal

> I've only cut myself once. 'Course, I've only shaved my legs once.

HERE'S THE DEAL ABOUT EYEBROWS

Who, ME?

I think MY eyebrows are _____.

How many times have I heard stories like these from tween girls?

> One time I thought my eyebrows looked too bushy, so instead of tweezers, I used little kid scissors. Yeah, it didn't turn out right. One eyebrow was practically gone, and the other one was still bushy. I didn't look at a mirror until it was back to normal.

> One time when I was about eleven, I tried to shape my eyebrows with a razor. My hand slipped when my sister knocked on the bathroom door, and not only did I cut my forehead, I shaved off a lot of my eyebrow. It took two months for the hair to grow back.

> **I didn't like my eyebrows because they were so thick, so I went after them with a pair of tweezers. It was hard to even them up, so I kept plucking until I had like a comma over each eye. For the next six months, I had to keep explaining why most of my eyebrows were missing. I don't recommend doing that.**

You might not have thought much about your eyebrows, unless ...

- you've found yourself with one big eyebrow going all the way across.

- you really want a polished, finished look.

If you do want to take out stray hairs or get rid of your uni-brow, follow these instructions very closely (and avoid the brow bummers your fellow mini-women ended up with!).

To make a space between eyebrows:

1. Take a shower, or wash your face with very warm water before you start. It won't sting as much when you pull out the hairs.

2. Use good tweezers with slanted ends, not the pointy kind. Save those for splinters.

3. Get close to the mirror. Better yet, use a hand mirror. BEST yet, use a magnifying mirror.

4. Simply pinch a hair with the tweezers, and give a sharp little tug. The hair should come right out.

Don't tweeze your brows any farther back than the inside corners of your eyes. If you get one eyebrow farther in than the other, don't try to even them out. You too could end up with little commas for eyebrows!

To make eyebrows look neat and groomed:

1. Following the same guidelines as the previous list, remove hairs that have popped in under your eyebrows.

2. Don't tweeze any above the brows at this point. It's too easy to wind up with thin lines instead of nice velvety, healthy-looking eyebrows.

Some "don'ts" for mini-woman eyebrows:

1. *Waxing.* Again, it can be painful and it costs money, and there IS the danger that too much eyebrow will be taken off. I advise you not to even go there right now.

2. *Shaving.* That's for legs and pits, not for brows. It's harder to get them looking right, you run the risk of nicking yourself, and they grow back as stubbly as legs do.

3. *Hair removal lotions and creams.* No matter what the label might say, the chemicals they contain are bad for your eyes. Really bad!

Just So You Know

Some girls get really self-conscious about dark hair on their arms. But there's no reason to try to remove it the way you do leg hair. It doesn't look unfeminine. If someone teases you about it, you can answer the way one mini-woman did: "I'm Italian, what can I say?"

YOU CAN DO IT

The very cool thing about having leg hair to shave and eyebrows to shape—or even knowing you will someday—is that it means you're turning into a young woman. The "Glad I'm a Girl Party" will give you (and your besties if you want) a chance to celebrate that. You can do the "Vision of Me-ness Collage" as part of your gala get-together or on your own—whatever works for you. At the end, you'll have a chance to make an entry in your travel journal.

What you'll need for the Glad I'm a Girl Party:

○ Other girls you like (or even just your BFF), unless you prefer to celebrate by yourself, which is fine too.

○ A place where you can totally be yourselves for an hour or two (Even a sleepover is a possibility.).

○ A few decorations to make the space female festive—balloons and butterflies, posters of your fave girl sports stars, whatever makes you feel like the girls you are (You can even ask each girl to bring her own fave girl thing.).

○ Snacks—some healthy, some treats, everything just the way you girls like it (don't forget the perfect plates and napkins).

○ Each girl's baby picture (obviously every guest will bring her own).

What you're doing:

You're getting together with other mini-women who are experiencing the frustration but also the fun of becoming the beautiful girls you were made by God to be. It's a time to celebrate whatever you think is GREAT about being a girl, whether that's "We get to wear cool clothes and hairstyles," "We get to play soccer for real," or "We're not boys!"

How to make it happen:

You can, of course, do whatever you want to celebrate your girl-icity, but these are a few suggestions to get your started:

○ If you've asked your friends to bring their fave girl thing for decoration, have each girl put her decoration on the table and explain why it shows what being a beautiful girl is to her.

○ Ask each girl to show her baby picture so you can all squeal over (a) how cute she was even back then and (b) how much more beautiful she is NOW.

○ Make "Vision of Me-ness Collages."

What you'll need for the Vision of Me-ness Collage:

○ lots of magazines you can cut up

○ a pair of scissors for each person

○ a glue stick for each person

○ a large piece of plain paper for each girl

What you're doing:

Each guest (or just you if you're doing this solo) is making a picture out of a lot of other pictures that will show how she feels about being a girl and what her unique girlness looks like.

How to make it happen:

1. Set a timer for fifteen minutes.

2. During that time, each person goes through the magazines and cuts out all the pictures and phrases and words that she likes, that strike her as being beautiful.

3. When the timer goes off, give each girl her large sheet of paper so she can arrange all the things she's collected any way she likes. In a collage, everything is usually touching and doesn't appear to have any particular design. It just all goes on there together.

4. Once the images are arranged, it's time to glue them on.

5. When everyone is finished, give each person a chance to show her collage and let the others describe what they see overall. Very romantic and soft? Active and wild? Totally organized? All about nature?

6. Then let the collage-creator herself describe what she sees. There are going to be some surprises.

You'll all be amazed at what you discover about your beautiful selves, which makes it a good time to break out the snacks and thank God for making you God's Girls.

When you're alone again, you can add another page to your travel journal (whatever you're calling it from chapter 11). Create a new page called "My Smooth Moves." Copy these headings onto the page, and fill in your information. Be as creative as you want, of course—and feel free to let that sense of humor out too!

My Hairy Leg Situation	My Eyebrow Situation
What I'll Do about That	**What to Do and When (if anything!)**

That's What I'm Talkin' About

Just as you've been doing at the ends of the previous chapters, journal or draw or simply think about how all the stuff you've just read applies to you. You can either fill in answers here or you can write/draw them on a page in your travel journal.

Here are this chapter's things to ponder when it's just you and God talkin':

My attitude about body hair is _____

_____.

When it comes to shaving or tweezing, I need to talk to my mom about _____

_____

_____.

I'd really like for my talks with my mom about stuff like this to be _____

_____.

Since God really does care about every part of me, I'd like to ask God this about the new body hair thing I'm going through: _____

_____

_____ ?

15

Things That Will Come in Handy and Footy!

It's a strange thing about hands and feet. When you're little, you don't even think about them. Then you hit someplace in your tween years, and you start saying things like these mini-women have shared with me:

> My feet are too big for how tall I am.

> My nails are so short they even look bad with polish on them.

> 66 I clean my feet, but they still always smell. 99

> 66 I am chewing my fingernails even as I'm writing this e-mail! 99

Yeah, this is one of those areas where it was definitely easier to be a little kid. And yet there's a positive side to your new awareness that, wow, you have fingers and toes to take care of too.

> 66 I love giving people manicures and pedicures and painting my own nails. That's the NICE part about being a girl! 99

> 66 I wear a size 9½ to 10 shoe and, honestly, I like having big feet. Makes me feel unique. 99

> 66 My mom is finally letting me use a lot of different colors of polish (although my dad still won't let me paint my nails black). 99

Who, ME?

Do you have a foot or hand problem that drives you nuts?

_____

_____

If you want to be a beautiful you (and obviously you do or you wouldn't still be reading!), your hands and feet will require some care. So that it won't be "one MORE thing I gotta do!" let's look at God's take on hands first.

GOT GOD?

God has plans for hands. Big plans. These are just a few of the ways they're used in the Bible to do God-things:

- **Appealing to God for help**—like Moses putting up his hands for God's power in battle (Exodus 17:11).

- **Healing**—like Jesus laying hands on people to cure them (Mark 5:23).

- **Working**—like the woman of noble character making clothes (Proverbs 31:24).

- **Helping**—like the Good Samaritan picking up and helping the guy everybody else left in the road (Luke 10:30–37).

- **Praying**—the way Jesus taught us to (Matthew 6:9–13).

What if you didn't do that because your hands didn't look like a nail-polish commercial? You'd be letting God and other people and yourself down, right? Since there are about a bajillion things you use your hands for, why not keep them looking at least clean and neat (if not downright fabulous)?

Have YOU ever hidden your hands because you thought they were nasty looking?

_____

_____

That Is SO Me!

Check yourself out, then.

When it comes to taking care of your hands, you can go from ...

Cleaner than
your brother's

Basically neat
and clean

A little polished
(and neat and clean)

A funky expression
of your wild self
(and neat and clean)

Circle the look that YOU would like to go for (even if you're not doing it now).

Remember that there's no right or wrong. If you can't see yourself spending your birthday money on a bottle of Sparkling Scarlet, basically keeping your hands and nails clean is fine, even for the rest of your life. If you get really jazzed about hand model nails, that's okay too.

Who, ME?

On a scale of 1 to 10 (ten being the best), how are YOUR hand-washing habits?

_____

Who, ME?

What's the strangest thing YOU have ever found under your fingernails?

_____

_____

Who, ME?

Use one word to describe the natural shape of YOUR nails.

_____

" I like my fingernails—when I can actually do something successful with nail polish. :) "

Just So You Know

Instead of shaking the bottle to mix polish, roll it between your palms a couple of times. That way you won't get bubbles on your nails.

HERE'S THE DEAL ABOUT HAND BASICS

No matter which of the four looks you circled, you'll need to follow the basics for taking care of your hands.

Hand Care Tip #1: Wash your hands. Duh-uh, right? But you'd be surprised how many people don't even think about it. Really clean your hands with warm water and soap (not just a quick run under the faucet before you take off). The bare minimum is to wash your hands when …

- You've just used the bathroom.

- You're about to eat (whether it's sticking your hand in a bag of chips or sitting down to a big dinner).

- You're getting ready to fix something to eat.

- You've been touching an animal.

- You've been shopping.

- Your hands feel sticky, greasy, grimy, or just a little icky.

- You have a cold (Wash your hands twice as much as usual and definitely after you've wiped your nose—hello-o!).

- You've been around somebody who's sick.

This makes it sound like you have to have your hands in the sink all the time, but once it becomes a habit, you won't feel that way. It can be hard to get to soap and water when you're in school all day, so keep some hand sanitizer or wipes in your backpack. If somebody calls you a clean freak, pass him a wet wipe.

Hand Care Tip #2: **Get the dirt out from under your fingernails.** Once a day, after you get out of the shower or tub, use a metal nail file (like the kind that comes on nail clippers) to gently scrape any leftover stuff from under your nails. Do it even if they don't look dirty. You'd be amazed what hides in there. (You don't really want to know …)

Hand Care Tip #3: **Moisturize.** Remember that from the skin chapter? When you're putting on lotion after your bath or shower, pay attention to your hands. This is especially important in cold climates where the temperatures can chap the skin on your hands just like it does your lips.

If you circled "Cleaner than your brother's" on "That Is SO Me!" you're done. You can move on to "Here's the Deal about Fingernail Issues."

If you circled "Basically neat AND CLEAN," there are a few more steps. The good news is you don't have to do these every day. For hands and nails that say, "This girl takes good care of herself," do the following once a week:

Hand Care Tip #4: **File your nails.** An emery board is a nail file that has really fine sandpaper on it. Don't file with the metal thing even though it's called a nail file. (Go figure!)

- Don't go back and forth like you're sawing a log. That's makes your nails weak. Start at one side of your nail and file in one direction toward the center, and then do the same from the other side.

- Since this takes time, you might do it while you're watching a movie or something.

- File until all your nails are the same length and shape, probably an oval or as close as you can get to that. You might have one or two nails that are nice and long and you're proud of them, but if the rest are way short, it's going to look funny. Say good-bye to the long ones, and file away.

Hand Care Tip #5: Take care of your cuticles. That's the skin around your nails that tends to creep onto them. It's healthier if they stay in place.

1. Soak your fingers in a little bowl of hot, soapy water for a few minutes to soften up your cuticles.

2. Using what's called an orange stick (a little wooden thing with a slanted end) or a cotton swab, gently push the cuticles off your nails. Think of it as gently persuading them to get back where they belong.

3. If any little pieces of cuticle stick up (like they're breaking off), you can clip them with tiny manicure scissors. Just to be on the safe side, have an experienced person (mom, big sister, etc.) show you how to do that. The broken cuticle is dead, but the skin that's still attached isn't. Nobody should bleed during a manicure!

That's it. Look at you. Nice hands, girlfriend.

If on "That Is SO Me!" you circled "A little polished,"

you need to do all of the above before you move on to this part. Putting nail polish on nails that are dirty and ragged is sort of like putting frosting on a cake that hasn't been baked, you know? Once you're ready, here's what to do to look a little polished in the nail department.

1. Remove all old polish. You'll just need cotton balls you can dip in nail polish remover. Wipe from bottom to top until it ALL comes off.

2. Use a clear coat of polish first. There are special base coats, or you can just use clear. This is important if you plan to paint your nails a lot, because without it, colored polish can make them look yellow after a while. Just use two or three strokes with the polish brush to cover your whole nail. That's all it takes. Any more and it gets gloppy.

3. Let that dry before you move on. Don't rush. If that looks nice to you, you can stop there. Clear polish doesn't show as much when it chips off, and your nails will look shiny and pretty.

4. Put on two layers of colored polish—if you want color. Again, just use two or three strokes and let them dry completely in between.

5. Apply a clear coat over the colored polish. That will help keep the color from chipping.

6. Don't do anything "nail intensive" for several hours, which means you might want to do your manicure before you go to bed. Don't let water touch them. Even if you speed dry by putting your hands in the freezer for two minutes, all the coats won't be

entirely dry for three hours. So if you don't go right to bed, at least don't fingerpaint, dig a hole, or enter a pie-eating contest!

7. When your polish starts to chip (and it will), remove it with nail polish remover. A flake of polish in the middle of each nail is definitely not a good look for anybody. Not a good idea to chip it off with your other nails or (yikes!) with your teeth. Wait until you have time to sit down with remover and cotton balls.

If on "That Is SO Me!" you circled "A funky expression of your wild self," do ALL of the previous steps above, except that when you get ready to polish, use your imagination! This is one form of makeup parents don't usually object to (although you'll want to check with yours first), and it can be a blast.

- **Find fun colors you like.** Nail polish can be pretty cheap to buy, and a bottle lasts a while. There are so many shades that come in everything from satiny to sparkly-like-metal. There's even glitter polish, which is TOO fun. Enjoy wild, strange nail color now, because as you get older, it won't be the thing to do.

- **Avoid fake nails.** You know, the kind you can buy in a package that you stick on with glue? That sticky stuff really isn't good for your nails. Who wants to look fake anyway, unless you're playing the wicked witch in the school play?

Who, ME?

Have YOU ever had a nail polish disaster?

_____

_____

_____

> If you're gonna do your nails, then do it over something like a paper towel on the table. It'll save you a mother/father/both yelling at you.

Who, ME?

If you could paint YOUR nails however you wanted, what would you do?

_____

_____

> Once I bought some kids' fake nails and put them on to go to a birthday party. Right in the middle of a game, a bunch of them popped off and my nails looked disgusting underneath. SOOOO embarrassing.

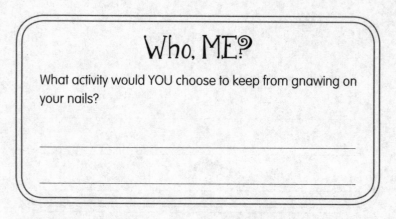

Who, ME?

What activity would YOU choose to keep from gnawing on your nails?

_____

_____

HERE'S THE DEAL ABOUT FINGERNAIL ISSUES

These are some questions mini-women ask a lot.

> I have really hard nails that can get long and I like them, but my mom makes me cut them all the time. What's up with that?

Long nails look glamorous in magazines, but they probably aren't the best idea for you right now because …

- They get in the way when you're writing, playing sports, or using the computer.

- They take a LOT of attention. (Do you have time for that? Seriously?)

- They look out of place when you're a tween (the way a lot of makeup does).

Just above the tip of your finger is probably long enough. Shorter is okay too.

> **My question is what is a way to stop biting nails?**

A lot of girls your age (and older!) chew their finger-nails. You probably aren't even aware that you're doing it; it's just that you get a little nervous or bored and before you realize it, you're down the quick. If you want to stop ...

- For a few days, pay attention to WHEN you bite.

- Try to find a substitute thing to do with your hands during those times (like knitting when you're watching TV or squeezing clay while you're studying for a test).

- Put some vinegar on your finger tips during those times to remind you when you unconsciously put them to your lips (just don't get it in your eyes or on the furniture or your clothes).

- Keep telling yourself that every time you stick your fingers in your mouth, you're feeding yourself germs. (That oughta do it!)

Now, how about those feet? Once again, we begin with God.

> **Some people think it's bad to have big feet or hands. But, really, they're parts of you too—so why not love them?**

GOT GOD?

Hands are one thing, but why would God care about your *feet*? Nobody can see them most of the time, so when it comes right down to it, why should *you* care that much about them either?

Actually, God's people talked about feet all the time in the Bible. Mostly they used them as symbols, in spite of their smelliness and fuzz between the toes—which just goes to show God can use anybody and anything! They represent ...

- Us standing up for what's right.

> He set my feet on a rock and gave me a firm places to stand.
>
> Psalm 40:2

- Us walking a path with God.

> Your word is a lamp for my feet, a light on my path.
>
> Psalm 119:105

- Us loving each other in a BIG way.

> "Now that I, your Lord and Teacher, have washed your feet, you also should wash one another's feet."
>
> John 13:14

Since we're talking about sacred symbols, it looks like we'd better be taking care of them, yes?

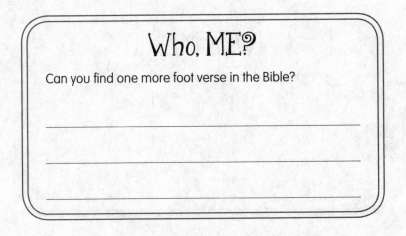

Who, ME?

Can you find one more foot verse in the Bible?

_____

_____

_____

HERE'S THE DEAL ABOUT FOOT CARE

You basically take care of your feet the same way you do your hands, with a few special variations.

Foot Fact #1: Since toenails are tougher than fingernails, you should trim them with clippers instead of trying to file them.

Foot Fact #2: It's better to cut your toenails straight across instead of making ovals. Otherwise, you can get ingrown toenails. (Trust me, you don't want those.)

Foot Fact #3: While you're doing your weekly manicure, soaking your feet in warm water will soften them up.

Foot Fact #4: You can use the pointed thing on the nail clippers to clean out the dirt from under your toenails. You think your *fingernails* get icky …

Foot Fact #5: If you're going to polish your toenails, you can put pieces of cotton between your toes to spread them out so you don't get polish all over them.

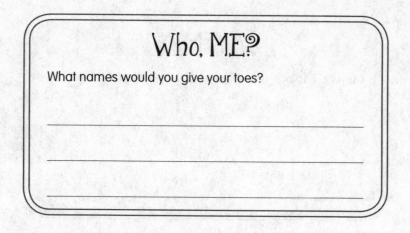

Who, ME?

What names would you give your toes?

_____

_____

_____

HERE'S THE DEAL ABOUT FOOT FUNKINESS

Once we get past "Ooh, feet—gross!" mini-women ask me these questions a *lot*.

> I don't like to wear flip-flops or go barefoot because I have (ugly) warts on my feet.

Warts are common, and you can get them on your hands too. Although they're not anybody's best look, they're harmless and usually go away.

- You can try treatments from the drugstore, but know that it takes a while for warts to shrivel up.

- If a wart is really bugging you, especially if it's on the bottom of your foot (a plantar wart), a doctor can "freeze" it off.

- And by the way, frogs and toads don't give you warts, so don't run screaming from them.

> **My feet smell so bad, I won't take my shoes off in front of people. That's kind of hard when I go to a sleepover.**

Yeah, feet can definitely get smelly. Once they do, you have to wash them to get rid of the stinkiness. Let's review the tips to prevent them from smelling up the place to begin with ...

- Wear socks made of natural fibers, like cotton, wool, or bamboo that absorb sweat before it causes yuckiness.

- Your shoes should be made of natural stuff too, such as leather or canvas. Plastic tennies and sandals may be fun, but, ooh, can they smell!

- If your shoes are giving off a less-than-delicious aroma, sprinkle baking soda inside them and leave it in overnight.

- Sneakers cause more of a stench than any other kind of shoe. If you have a big problem with stinky feet, switch to sandals or loafers or cute flats when you can.

> **Why do I keep getting blisters on my feet?**

If you get blisters or you can't wait to take your shoes off, you're probably wearing shoes that don't fit well. Your feet are growing right now, so have your feet measured every time you go shopping for shoes. And don't beg for the pair you love if the store doesn't have your size.

> **I would feel so much more girly if I could wear higher heels, but my mom won't let me.**

Yeah, you need to listen to her, because ...

- Three-inch heels when you're ten are right up there with the glamour nails and the heavy eye shadow we've been talking about. They make you look like you're playing dress up with your mom's shoes.

- High heels throw your spine completely out of line and cause all kinds of problems with hips, knees, and even necks. They're cool for special occasions as you get older, but never for all day.

So be part of the generation that says, "We will NOT walk around on stilts! We will take care of our bodies!"

> **What's with the fungus between my toes?**

Those red, scaly patches are called athlete's foot, though you don't have to be an athlete to get it. To avoid it ...

- Wear flip-flops when you take a shower in a locker room or at a pool, since that's where we usually pick up the fungus.

- Dry your feet really well after a bath, and don't wear the same shoes all the time.

- If you do get athlete's foot, start treating it with a powder, spray, or cream you can get at the drugstore. It won't go away by itself, and who wants itchy feet 24/7?

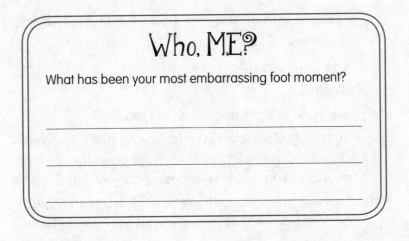

Who, ME?

What has been your most embarrassing foot moment?

_____

_____

_____

YOU CAN DO IT

By this time you might be thinking that doing the beauty thing is a lot of work! You've got your hair to take care of. Your skin. Your hands. Even your toenails. How are you even supposed to remember all that stuff, much less do it?

Let's stop and take care of that right now by making a beauty chart to help you keep track of what to do and when. You can include it as a new page in your travel journal, or make it big enough to hang on your wall.

What you'll need for your beauty chart:

○ a piece of poster board, poster-sized paper, or four sheets of regular paper taped together to make one big square (if you want your chart to hang on the wall); OR (if you want to put your chart in your travel journal) an 11" by 14" piece of paper you can fold in half and slip inside the journal when it's done

○ a yardstick or ruler

○ a pencil

○ markers, colored pencils, or crayons

○ anything else you want to use to decorate your chart (stickers, stars, pictures from magazines, even photos of you doing your beauty-care thing)

○ tacks (if you want to hang your chart, with Mom's permission) or that gummy stuff you use to hang posters

How to make it happen:

There is no right or wrong way for your chart to look, so be creative. This process is easiest. (The ones with stars beside them are the optional items. Include those on your chart only if you're really into them.)

○ Write these down the left side of your paper or poster board:

  ○ **EVERY DAY OR TWO DAYS**
  - wash body
  - wash hair
  - use conditioner*
  - shave legs and pits*
  - comb wet hair
  - use body lotion
  - clean under fingernails
  - drink at least four glasses of water

338

- wash hands often

○ **EVERY MORNING**

- wash face
- use moisturizer with sunscreen
- brush hair
- style hair

○ **EVERY NIGHT**

- wash face
- use moisturizer
- brush hair
- get eight hours sleep

○ **WEEKLY**

- soak feet
- remove old nail polish*
- file nails
- take care of cuticles
- clean under toenails
- clip toenails
- put on new polish*

○ **EVERY SIX WEEKS**

- have hair trimmed

○ Across the top, write two months' worth of dates, so that you form columns for checking things off. (You've seen charts like this in school a bunch, right?)

○ Using your ruler or yardstick, draw lines across for each item and down for each date, making boxes. Decorate your chart however you want to.

○ Find a good place to hang your chart so you'll remember to check items off each day/week. Or, if you've made a small one, keep it in your "travel journal" so you can mark it daily, just by folding it out.

○ You can make check marks with a cool pen or marker, or you can use stars, stickers, or smiley faces—whatever makes it fun for you to keep track of the good care you're taking of your beautiful self.

It's very cool to watch yourself form habits. Remember, though, that if you miss a day doing one of your beauty tasks, it doesn't mean you're going to be ugly that day! Just get back on track the next day.

That's What I'm Talkin' About

As always, you can either fill in your answers here or you can write/draw them on a page in your travel journal.

Here are this chapter's things to ponder when it's just you and God talkin':

Now I would describe my hands as being _____

_____.

And my feet as being _____

_____.

I think I'll be _____

about keeping up with my Beauty Chart because _____

_____

_____.

This week I'm going to use my (beautiful) hands to do this

God-thing: _____

_____

And my (beautiful) feet to do this God-thing: _____

_____

_____

16

Stylin'

When I asked the mini-women in my tween you and me blog to comment about clothes, the inbox filled up mega-fast. I got everything from ...

"I am SO into the fashion thing. I think about clothes all the time. I DREAM about clothes!"

to ...

"I HATE shopping for clothes. I hate even thinking about clothes. It's a total waste of time."

Unless you've been a fashionista since you were a toddler (and some girls are from the time they can say the word "shoe"), you might just now be starting to get more interested in your wardrobe. As one tween put it, *"I used to not think much about what I wore at all, but*

I've been realizing that I'm taking a bigger notice as I'm getting older."

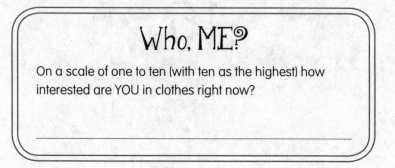

Who, ME?

On a scale of one to ten (with ten as the highest) how interested are YOU in clothes right now?

_____

There is no "normal" when it comes to clothes. (You probably could've guessed I'd say that!) In fact, this is the appearance area where you can do the **most** to express your real self, and that's what this chapter is all about. Even if you're like the mini-woman who said, *"I usually wear just a T-shirt and jeans, and it suits me fine,"* this can be fun for you. After all, who doesn't want to show that she's for real? That's actually what God the Great Designer wants from us.

> We can worship God by wearing clothes that aren't way-tight. Especially bikinis.

GOT GOD?

If you read all the Bible verses about clothes, at first you might think God can't make up his mind about what we're supposed to wear! Let's take them one at a time and see what God really has to say.

- **God does want you to look your best.** The woman of noble character described in Proverbs "is clothed in fine linen and purple" (Proverbs 31:22). That doesn't mean you have to wear the most expensive labels and always look like you just walked out of Justice. It means that when you put on clothes that look good and feel great on you, **that** says, "I want people to see the real me, a person who deserves respect."

- **"Best" in God's eyes, is different for everyone**. And not only does God create you to be one of a kind, but he also watches you with loving eyes, coaxing you to be who he made you to be. "[God] forms the hearts of all ... considers everything they do" (Psalm 33:15).

Does it make sense, then, that everybody should dress exactly the same? It's totally natural to want the clothes "everybody" is wearing because you want to feel like part of a group. But it's also a time for learning what makes you unique because it makes you a valuable part of that group. Your best look is clothes that match that.

- **God doesn't want you to get all freaked out about what you're going to wear**. Jesus talked about that in his famous Sermon on the Mount.

> "See how the flowers of the field grow. They do not labor or spin. Yet I tell you that not even Solomon in all his splendor was dressed like one of these. If that is how God clothes the grass of the field ... will he not much more clothe you?"
>
> Matthew 6:28–30

He wasn't saying we can just step out of the shower and God will put clothes on us.

He meant that clothes shouldn't be the most important thing on the entire planet in our minds. It's fun to have a trendy belt or the everybody-has-them jeans. It's also fun to play board games, stay up late giggling, and make valentines for the patients at the nursing home. It's all about balance. Look good and then get on with the other stuff.

- **God is way more interested in how we live than how we dress**, because that's what truly makes us beautiful. This is kind of a no-brainer, but which of these choices do you think is more important to God:

  ○ What shoes I wear or how I treat my mom?

  ○ Whether I have a way-cool swimsuit or whether I'm nice to the school "outcasts"?

  ○ Which top I wear with which jeans or what I say to my friend who's having a bad day?

So what does all of that mean for your wardrobe? Pick out clothes that …

1. help you feel like you're part of the group.

2. allow you to be your unique self.

3. aren't the center of your universe.

4. allow your natural, inner beauty to shine through.

How are you going to do all that at the same time? Fortunately, God doesn't ask us to do the impossible, so let's find out.

Just So You Know

If you're focusing on who you really are, you won't have to worry about whether you're dressing modestly or not. "Showing off your body" isn't who anybody IS, so you naturally won't even go there.

Who, ME?

Which one of those four things on page 346 do YOU need the most help with?

_____

That Is SO Me!

Have you ever felt like you were wearing somebody else's clothes? That's probably because what you had on didn't tell who you were. The first step is to find your personal style.

Circle one item in each list that comes closest to something YOU would like to do (even if you never have).

(a) play softball	(b) play Scrabble	(c) play a pretend
(a) have a pillow fight	(b) do a magazine quiz	(c) giggle and talk with friends
(a) ride my bike	(b) read a book	(c) dream up a story
(a) play a computer game	(b) check out a Web site	(c) e-mail a friend

| (a) try snow boarding | (b) build the perfect snowman | (c) watch the snow fall |

Now count up your a's, b's, and c's and enter the numbers here:

- _____ a's

- _____ b's

- _____ c's

Did you have more a's than other letters? You may prefer the sporty casual style. Who can do all the moving around you like to do in dresses and skinny jeans and pointy-toed shoes? Go with clothes that are comfortable and fun, even when you have to get dressed up. You can never tell when somebody might want to race you or there's a tree that has to be climbed …

More b's than other letters? Using your mind makes you happy, so you might really like a classic, tailored style. Not dull, of course, but crisp lines and cool jackets and pants and skirts you can mix 'n' match. Smart clothes!

If you scored highest in c's, you probably enjoy quiet, dreamy things. Yours is more than likely an all-girl romantic style. It's fashion that fits your imaginative self— maybe embroidery on your jeans, spangles on your purse, beads on your flip-flops. And loads of pastels?

What if you had an almost-equal number of each letter? You are a girl with many sides, which means your style is creative and unpredictable. You like to be a tomboy one day and a girly-girl the next and keep everybody guessing. Go ahead and combine more than one style at a time: clunky boots with a long flowy skirt, or a baseball cap with sequins on it.

Write your style here (and be proud of it!)

_____

66 I would describe my style as boyish but with my own personal additions. 99

66 Some people might say my style is punky because it's bright, out-there, and different. Like my favorite outfit is my neon green plaid pants with my black high tops and my black shirt that says 'Chillin' Peeps' on the front, with my fingerless gloves and my black and white fedora. 99

66 If you look good in jeans, wear them. They look good with almost every shirt, and if you have a dress that's too short, just put on jeans under it. 99

66 I love designing my own clothes and making them—I LOVE that! Then what I wear isn't like what anybody else is wearing. 99

Who, ME?

The best pants for me would be …

_____

_____

_____

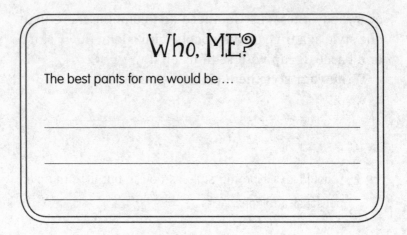 I just mostly wear T-shirts and sweatshirts and jeans, but my shirts usually say stuff about me. I have lots of horse shirts, and I love the one that says, 'Here's one girl who would rather be trotting than texting.'

Who, ME?

If I could have a perfect-for-me top right now, it would be …

_____

_____

_____

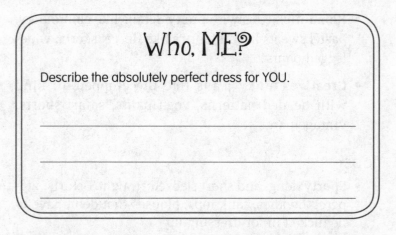

Who, ME?

Describe the absolutely perfect dress for YOU.

_____

_____

_____

HERE'S THE DEAL ABOUT YOUR STYLE

Being sporty, tailored, romantic, or creative doesn't mean you have to dress like that all the time. Maybe this time next year you'll change styles completely as you find out more about who you are. But since most of us don't have unlimited funds to spend on our wardrobes, it's best to make sure most of your clothes are the usual you.

Here are some suggestions to help you shop, either at the store or in your own closet.

Pants

- **Sporty**: your favorite style jeans, fun sweats, cargo pants, easy-to-move-in shorts, dressier pants in great colors for special occasions

- **Tailored**: crisp jeans that fit well, your favorite style khakis, sweats that have matching jackets, shorts with belts 'n' pockets, dressier pants that look fabulous with boots or slip-on flats

- **Romantic**: jeans with pretty details like embroidery, pastel sweats in soft fabrics like fleece, skorts, wide-legged pants

- **Creative**: funky jeans like the cropped-off kind with beaded patterns, yoga pants, safari shorts, vintage pants

Tops

- **Sporty**: long- and short-sleeved straight T-shirts, zippered hoodies, tank tops, blouses that don't have to be tucked in for dressing up

- **Tailored**: long and fitted T-shirts, turtleneck and crewneck sweaters, fresh-looking sleeveless blouses, fitted blouses with details like tucks and pleats for dress up

- **Romantic**: long- and short-sleeved T-shirts with girly details like glitter, "fancy" sweaters, peasant blouses, empire-waist tops for dress up

- **Creative**: long- and short-sleeved T-shirts with unusual designs on them, bulky knit sweaters and ponchos, tanks tops that look like two, tunic tops with fun details for dress up

Skirts and Dresses

- **Sporty**: khaki and denim A-line skirts, skorts, simple dresses in fabrics that breathe (like 100 percent cotton)

- **Tailored**: straight and pleated skirts; long skirts with simple lines; dresses with belts, pockets, and collars

- **Romantic**: skirts that swirl when you twirl; gathered

skirts; dresses with sashes, pretty sleeves, and details at the hem

- **Creative**: skirts with unexpected features like shiny beads on denim or oversized pockets; wrap-around skirts; dresses that look like they might have come from another country

Jackets or Coats (depending on where you live)

- **Sporty**: jean jackets, down jackets, parkas, sweater-jackets
- **Tailored**: blazers, peacoats, fitted ski jackets, long coats with simple lines
- **Romantic**: short (to the waist) jackets, furry jackets and coats, pastel ponchos
- **Creative**: unusual jean jackets, colorful ponchos, bomber jackets, capes and shawls

> My friend thinks that you can only be cool if you wear the latest trends. Only ... right now what's in isn't me and it definitely doesn't FIT.

It can feel like if you don't wear the most up-to-the-minute outfits, you're a loser. I'm going to let your fellow mini-women help you out with that.

> No offense, but other people are SO not the clothing police.

66 Clothes are a big deal to the popular girls in my school, but not to my friends and me, and that's okay. 99

66 Despite what other people say, you don't have to be 'struttin' your stuff' to be beautiful or cute. Who even came up with that ridiculousness anyway? You should draw more attention to your face and how much your style represents who you are, who God made you to be, than to your body and how badly you want to be noticed. 99

66 Clothes are just FABRIC, so you shouldn't bother about what everybody's wearing. 99

66 If you judge people by the way they dress, you're going to miss who they really are inside. 99

I'll just add one more thing. Always ask yourself, *does God want to see me in this?*

Enough said?

Who, ME?

What's your favorite jacket or coat you've ever bundled up in?

_____

_____

Who, ME?

If YOU could start your OWN fashion trend, what would it be?

_____

_____

That Is SO Me!

Have you ever **really** wanted something everybody was wearing, and when you tried it on, it pulled in weird places? Or made you look, well, funny?

That's because there are different **body shapes**, and not every piece of clothing looks good on every one of them. Keeping in mind that God created—and loves—all shapes and sizes of people, let's discover what yours is right now.

Decide which one of these is closest to what YOU see when you look in a full-length mirror, wearing either your undies or clothes that fit pretty snugly. Write "ME!" on the space provided.

- _____ I'm medium to tall and sort of willowy. (Long and lean)

- _____ I'm short and pixie-ish, like I could be a real-life Tinkerbell. (Small and slim)

- _____I'm medium to tall, and I'm strong, like a one-woman powerhouse. (Athletic build with some curves)

- _____I'm short and sturdy, like an undercover superheroine. (Athletic build without curves)

- _____I'm medium to tall and curvy, like a young woman about to burst through. (Hourglass)

- _____I'm short and cuddly like a favorite teddy bear. (Soft and round)

Who knew there could be so many body types? The good news is, there are clothes for every body type. The bad news is ... well, there is no bad news!

Just So You Know

Your body shape will probably change some during your tween years, so even though I suggest ways to tone down body features you aren't crazy about, try not to get all worked up about a rounded tummy or the fact that you're the tallest one in the class. Your body is busy becoming its beautiful self.

Who, ME?

Draw a star next to the choice YOU are making.

HERE'S THE DEAL ABOUT DRESSING FOR YOUR BODY TYPE

Do you want to show your body type just as it is? OR Do you want to coax it to look even more beautiful?

There's no right or wrong answer. It's totally up to you as long as you like what you see when you get dressed and look in the mirror—because God wants us to do our personal best with what he's given us.

- **To play up your long, lean form**

  - **Do** think long and straight and try things that flow.

  - **Don't** choose belts at your waist or fabrics with big designs all over.

- **To look taller than you are**

  - **Do** wear the same color from top to bottom or pick vertical stripes.

  - **Don't** wear patterns that go sideways.

- **To play up how tiny you are**

  - **Do** keep your skirts above your knees (with Mom's approval).

  - **Don't** wear huge patterns. (They will wear you!)

- **To look shorter than you are**

  - **Do** keep your skirts at or below your knees; wear things that "cut you in half," like a different color on top than on the bottom.

  - **Don't** wear shoes with higher heels.

- **To put the focus on your strong, sturdy body**

  - ○ **Do** wear clothes that cling a little, and try stand-up collars and straight-leg pants.

  - ○ **Don't** think everything you wear has to be boyish.

- **To soften your sturdiness a little**

  - ○ **Do** wear clothes that are fitted (but not tight) and go for a small touch of girly detail, like some embroidery on a jeans pocket.

  - ○ **Don't** wear "boxy" clothes.

- **To enjoy your curves and fluffiness**

  - ○ **Do** go for loose-fitting things like full blouses and wide-legged pants.

  - ○ **Don't** think you can't be feminine!

- **To appear more streamlined**

  - ○ **Do** choose tops, dresses, and jackets that curve in at the waist.

  - ○ **Don't** wear things that are either too tight or too loose.

> **"** I have big, muscular legs from playing sports, and they look REALLY big in skinny jeans, so I don't wear them. **"**

Who, ME?

What article of clothing do you own that is totally YOU?

_____

_____

Just So You Know

What size clothes you wear isn't even worth talking about. Just buy things that fit you so that you can move freely and do all the fun stuff you like to do.

That Is SO Me!

One of the most fun things about clothes is that they come in so many different **colors**. Since _we_ come in so many different colors too, that's a good thing! It's amazing how the shades you were born to wear can make your natural beauty shine. Want to find your color code?

Take a good long look in a mirror in good light, and maybe ask your mom or another grown-up to consult with you. Then circle one description in each column that is _most_ like you. (We haven't covered all the possibilities, so if you want to write some things in, feel free.)

Hair	Skin
reddish	on the light side
blondish	on the dark side
dark	

Now check your unique (and beautiful!) combination:

- _____ reddish hair/light skin

- _____ blondish hair/light skin

- _____ blondish hair/dark skin

- _____ dark hair/light skin

- _____ dark hair/dark skin

Who, ME?

What's YOUR all-time fave color to wear?

_____

Who, ME?

What new color are YOU going to try?

_____

Just So You Know

You can't go wrong if you match your clothes to the color of your eyes.

HERE'S THE DEAL ABOUT DRESSING FOR YOUR COLORING

Of course, wear any color you want that makes you happy. God created a whole rainbow of hues for us to enjoy. If you really want to bring out the beauty of your natural coloring, here are some suggestions. Get ready to dazzle yourself!

	Best Colors	Not So Wonderful
Red hair/light skin	any shade of green or soft gold	blue, warm red, white, yellow, very pastel colors
Blondish hair/light skin	pink, light blue, violet, coral	light green, red, green, black, yellow, very pastel colors
Blondish hair/dark skin	white, pink, lavender,	light green, purple orange, neon colors
Dark hair/light skin	red, maroon, orange,	deep pink, beige, very pastel colors
Dark hair/dark skin	rich red, black, brown, bright blue, red	purple, emerald green, yellow, neon colors

Color can have an influence on your mood and on the way people see you. How cool is that?

- Need a little energy or a confidence boost? Wear **red**.

- Need to feel like you have it together? **White** is your best bet.

- Need to state your independence? Put on your **green**.

- Need to stay calm? Clothe yourself in **light blue**.

- Need to be taken seriously? Get into your **dark blue**.

- Need to be a little mysterious? **Black** is a good choice.

- Need a hug or really want someone to trust you? Wear **pastels** (light shades of soft color).

Who, ME?

What color should YOU wear tomorrow?

_____

66 I'm starting to care about clothes a little more. When I'm out walking my dog at our apartment complex, I watch people and wonder what I'd look like in some of their outfits. 99

Who, ME?

Circle the accessories on the list below that YOU like to wear/use.

HERE'S THE DEAL ABOUT ACCESSORIZING

The absolutely most fun thing about putting an outfit together is adding the accessories. You know ...

great hats

cool scarves

fun jewelry

unusual belts

unique purses

funky socks and tights

and (of course!) shoes

Accessories are the magic in your wardrobe. They can ...

- turn a few basic items of clothing into a whole bunch of different outfits.

- draw attention to your best features.

- draw the focus away from things you're self-conscious about.

- let you express your unique self in some fun ways.

There are certain things that draw attention wherever you put them ...

- bright, warm colors like yellow, red, orange, and gold

- big designs

- sparkly, shiny things

- girly details

Wear these attention getters near your best features ...

- Do you have great hair? Bring out the barrettes, the hair clips, and the funky scarves.

- Have a tiny waist? Put on those belts, baby.

- Really well-toned arms? Play them up with fun bracelets.

- Nice neck? Necklaces were made for you.

- Lovely legs? Go for the unique shoes, the perfect socks.

If you have a physical feature you're not so crazy about, keep the attention-getters away from there (but keep learning to accept that the way you were made is perfect in God's eyes).

- Self-conscious about your ears? Not the best place for flashy jewelry, right?

- Feeling like your hips are huge? (They probably aren't!) Don't hang a belt or scarf around them.

- Always want to hide your fingernails? Stay away from rings. (Or go back to chapter 15!)

And don't forget to show your true self when you're using accessories. Going back to your personal style, think about what is YOU. Here are some suggestions, but your own imagination is your best guide.

- **Sporty**: ball caps, visors, pendants of your favorite sports teams, canvas shoulder bags, fun backpacks, the most perfect socks you can find, tennis shoes with personality

- **Tailored**: sleek hats, wool scarves, gloves, simple jewelry, purses to match your shoes, touches of fun in belts and buttons and socks

- **Romantic**: sun hats, fuzzy winter caps with matching scarves and gloves, dainty jewelry (wherever you can hang it!), bows, lace, sparkly purses

- **Creative**: berets, newsboy caps, chunky jewelry, belts and scarves galore (worn in unexpected places), fun purses, colored shoes

Who, ME?

What's your best feature?

_____

Got an accessory for that?

_____

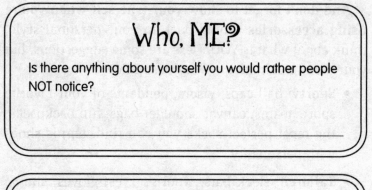

Who, ME?

Is there anything about yourself you would rather people NOT notice?

_____

Who, ME?

What one accessory that YOU own shouts, "This is ME!"

_____

" My mom and I argue sometimes because I don't put a jacket on 'completely' and she says it looks 'sloppy.' **"**

" I've only argued with my mom about clothes once, when I wanted this top that my mom said made me look like a 'bad girl.' She won. **"**

" My parents and I almost never have disagreements about clothes. I know what they approve of, and I'm not about to cross their boundaries. **"**

> 66 My mom got me a whole bunch of cute clothes, but most of the time I just want to wear a T-shirt. I go to a co-op where all the girls my age wear T-shirts. How do I tell my mom? 99

HERE'S THE DEAL ABOUT MOMS (AND DADS!) AND CLOTHES

> 66 My mom and I can never agree about clothes. When we go shopping, it's like one big fight the whole time. 99

Okay, so, yeah, decisions about what clothes are bought for you are up to the grown-ups in your family. But YOU can keep those decisions from turning into battles by following some of these tips. Someday you'll be using your own money for your wardrobe, so these are good **shopping skills** to learn for the future too.

Shopping Skill #1: Know how much money there is to spend, and don't try to persuade your folks to go outside their budget. You can pretty much tell what the finances are at your house, so why try to wheedle an expensive pair of jeans out of your mom when you know things are tight? If this is hard for you, try earning some money to buy a few things yourself. When you have to fork over your own cash for that new have-to-have-it, you might find out you really *don't* have to have it after all.

Shopping Skill #2: Ask your parents what things they will absolutely not allow you to wear, and then don't even go to those racks in the store. They'll be impressed with how mature you are.

Shopping Skill #3: Look for things that will go with what you already have. You might want new colors too, but be sure to choose things that will mix and match.

Shopping Skill #4: If you're dying for something trendy, suggest to your parents that you buy it at one of the less expensive stores. That way if you only wear it until it goes out of style (like maybe next month), it won't be a huge waste of money.

Shopping Skill #5: Remember that it's better to have a few perfect-for-you, good-quality pieces of clothing than a whole closet full of stuff that really isn't your best look. You can create different outfits just by changing accessories. And besides, what rule says you have to wear something different every single day? If it's great on you this Tuesday, it will still look fabulous next Tuesday!

Who, ME?

Draw an arrow next to each Shopping Skill in the previous list that YOU are going to work on.

YOU CAN DO IT

Now that you know all this cool stuff about enhancing your unique beauty with clothes and accessories, it's hard not to think, "I need to go shopping!" Actually, you don't. You can "shop" in your own closet and dresser drawers with **shop-at-home**. The results, as well as some dreams and plans, can go in your travel journal. And you're going to feel more like the beautiful you every minute!

What you'll need to Shop-at-Home:

- ○ about an hour of free time (more if you want)
- ○ all the clothes and accessories you own (But don't take them all out of the drawers and closets yet!)
- ○ a box or plastic bag for the giveaways
- ○ optional: index cards (in different colors if you're REALLY the organized type)

What you're doing:

You're discovering that you probably already own what you need to step out as your most beautiful self AND that you can put together way more outfits than you ever thought possible—all without spending a dime.

How to make it happen:

Step One: Put all your clothes in two piles …

- ○ things that don't fit you or have never been and will never be YOU. Ask if you can give them to charity. (Or your little sister!)
- ○ things that fit and have possibilities for your style, body type, and coloring.

Step Two: Pick up each item in the I'm-keeping-it pile and make a plan for it.

- ○ See how many other things it goes with.
- ○ Have fun putting surprising colors next to each other.

○ Use accessories to bring colors together. (Purple pants will go with a yellow top if you have a yellow and purple bracelet to tie them in.)

○ If it isn't exactly your style, see what you can put with it to capture the real you. (You may not be into that romantic pink skirt, but put on a jean jacket and some clean tennies—and you're your sporty self.)

Step Three: **If you REALLY love putting outfits together, write the combinations you discover on separate cards and pick one when it's time to get dressed.**

○ You can even put different types of outfits on different color cards—pink for dressing up, yellow for school ...)

○ If you would rather have your tonsils out than do that, just put like things together in the closet or in your drawers so it's easy for you to grab an outfit and go.

Now you can create a new page in your travel journal called "Dressing to Be Me." Copy these headings below onto the page and fill in the information. Be as creative as you want, of course—and feel free to include magazine pics or drawings of outfits you dream up (if that's YOUR thing).

> **Basic Items to Add to My Wardrobe**
> **Color**
> **What I Have That Will Go With It**
> **My Accessories That Will Work With It**

That's What I'm Talkin' About

This chapter's things to ponder (and draw or write about) when it's just you and God talkin':

I think from now on, getting dressed is going to be ____

_____

_____.

I've changed my clothes-attitude about _____

_____

_____

_____.

When it comes to clothes, I think God wants me to ___

_____

_____

_____.

I need to talk to my mom about _____

_____

_____

_____.

17

Don't You Hate That?

I like to focus on the positive, the things we can celebrate about the way we look. Still, it helps to be honest about the things we're *not* so happy about so we can deal with those too, right?

When I ask mini-women like you what bugs them about their appearance, they say:

"I am way taller than anybody!"

"I think my cheeks are way too fat."

"My stomach pokes out. I have a muffin top."

"I hate wearing glasses."

"I get teased because I'm 'underdeveloped.'"

Our goal is to get to the place on our journey where we can *honestly* say, "I feel beautiful just the way I am." But when a "beauty bummer" taunts you every time you look in the mirror, it can be hard to reach that place. That's what this chapter is about.

So if you're ready, let's start with how you feel right now.

That Is SO Me!

Here's a list of beauty bummers some mini-women say they'd rather live without. Look at each bummer and put a check mark if you have that particular thing in your life.

Then, if you do, circle the choice that best describes how you feel about it.

Remember, the quiz won't help you if you aren't honest ...

_____ **Glasses**

  ○ a. I absolutely hate them.

  ○ b. They're ... okay.

  ○ c. They're so ME!

  ○ d. What glasses?

_____ **Braces**

  ○ a. I'm counting the days until I get them off.

  ○ b. I don't really mind them most of the time.

  ○ c. It's actually cool to have braces.

  ○ d. What's the big deal?

_____ **Being Tall**

○ a. I feel like a giraffe.

○ b. It's not *that* bad.

○ c. Are you kidding? We tall girls look so good in our clothes!

○ d. Does anybody care?

_____ **Being Big**

○ a. It's so embarrassing to be huge.

○ b. I don't know; I guess it's just the way I am.

○ c. There's so much more of me to love!

○ d. So what?

_____ **Scars, Birthmarks, or Moles**

○ a. I wish I could just put a bag over my head.

○ b. People who know me get used to it.

○ c. I'm one of a kind!

○ d. I forgot about it until just now.

_____ **Other Physical Features Kids Tease You About**

○ a. I'm totally having plastic surgery when I turn eighteen.

○ b. Whatever. They'll grow up someday.

○ c. I inherited it, and I'm proud of it!

○ d. I don't even get why they tease me.

Even if you didn't have any check marks, read on anyway. Every girl has to deal with something she doesn't like about herself at some point. Besides, this chapter will show you how to help a girlfriend who might be struggling with a beauty bummer right now.

If you circled any a's, you're having a hard time, aren't you? People can be mean (or at least thoughtless), and as we've said, the world in general can make you think you have to be perfect. As you read on, remember that you're already beautiful and getting more so every day.

Did you circle some b's? If so, whatever some people consider a bummer doesn't really bother you that much. Wouldn't it be fun, though, to make it one of the best things about you? Read on!

If any c's are circled, you probably could have written this chapter yourself! You have the right idea. Keep reading so you can have even more fun with your unique look and encourage other girls to do the same. You can make a difference.

If you circled any d's, you don't even see any of this as a problem. Very cool. We would tell you not to even bother with this chapter, except that it will help you understand why other girls get upset. The last thing you want to do is tell a friend who's stressing about her glasses or her warts to "just get over it." But if you read on, you can *help* her accept all of herself, just the way you do.

We have our work cut out for us, so let's get started.

> ❝I used to worry I wasn't flat-chested enough (breasts don't look good in a leotard and I'm a dancer), but then I figured worrying about it or looking in the mirror won't change it, so why waste my time?❞

HERE'S THE DEAL ABOUT CHANGING

No matter what letters you circled in "That Is SO Me!" there are three things EVERYBODY needs to learn:

- how to know what you can change and what you can't.

- how to change what can be changed, or at least make it a little better.

- how to accept what can't be changed and maybe even make it work for you.

For example, let's say you have what you consider to be the longest nose in the galaxy, and other kids call you Pinocchio until you want to smack somebody. Consider the three questions.

Can I change it? Not unless you have plastic surgery ... Besides, who knows? Your face may grow into your nose and make you look fabulous.

How can I make it a little better? Wear your hair parted on the side and not too flat on top. Choose colors that bring out the color of your eyes.

How can I accept it and make it work for me? It's

probably a family trait, so be proud of that. Instead of thinking of it as "honkin' huge," find another way to describe it. Is it noble? Strong? Comical? Queenly? Call it that in your mind, and it will change everything, especially when somebody thinks he's original and calls you Pinocchio for the forty-fifth time.

Get the idea? Let's see what you can do with the basic beauty bummers to bring out more of that beautiful you.

GLASSES

Can I change it? Not unless you want to ruin your eyesight. There's nothing beautiful about squinting your eyes to see.

How can I make it a little better? Take your time picking out frames you like that look great on you. There's a shape and color and style for every person. Ask the folks at the optical store to help you find the perfect ones. Contact lenses are a choice, and they actually help you see better than glasses do. Just remember that they require a lot of care, are easy to lose, and are sometimes hard to get used to. You might want to wait until you're older.

How can I accept it and make it work for me? Think about having fewer headaches and getting better grades because you can actually see! Remember that glasses make a person look really smart. Make yours a part of your unique style, and people will say, "You look so much cuter with your specs on."

BRACES

Can I change it? Probably not, especially if you really

have some teeth and jaw issues that can affect your health.

How can I make it a little better? Braces and rubber bands come in different colors as well as in clear and silver. How fun is that? You can't hide them, so why not let them sparkle? To get those braces off as fast as you can (the average time to wear them is two and a half years), brush, floss, and avoid super hard or sticky, gooey foods.

How can I accept it and make it work for me? Your teeth are going to be amazing when you get the braces off, and that will last for the rest of your life. And you certainly aren't alone. How many other girls in your grade are wearing them and looking adorable? The best thing you can do is smile big and bright. You'll be unforgettable.

BEING TALL

Can I change it? Not a chance.

How can I make it a little better? Remember the advice in chapter 16 about what to wear? You'll still be the same height, but you can **look** shorter if you really want to.

How can I accept it and make it work for me? There are almost no minuses in being tall and lots of pluses. You look wonderful in clothes. Women who are tall are often automatically respected and considered to be leaders by other people. In a very short time, you'll really grow into your height and feel less gangly and klutzy. Meanwhile, you could learn to play basketball and volleyball. Dream of being a model. Enjoy the view. And most of all, stand up straight and proud.

BEING "BIG"

Can I change it? You can't change the fact that you have big, healthy bones and a strong frame. You can keep from being overweight, but you'll probably never be ultra-thin—and why would you want to be? You would look pretty funny with no meat on those wonderful bones!

How can I make it a little better? Go back to chapter sixteen to look at what clothes can soften your look a little. Be sure to eat good healthy stuff rather than junk and fast food. Get lots of fun exercise at least five times a week.

How can I accept it and make it work for me? You're strong and robust. That's a great look! People seem to trust those who are bigger than they are, so let your friends have confidence in you. Be comfortable in your own skin. You can make a difference, because people will always notice you. Live large!

SCARS, BIRTHMARKS, OR MOLES

Can I change it? Sometimes you can. Usually removing or toning down these kinds of things involves a doctor. Talk honestly with your parents about how you feel and how much you're being teased.

How can I make it a little better? Trying to cover up things like birthmarks or moles usually only draws attention to them. If you have a scar, ask your mom if you can use a little stick foundation in a yellow (not pink) tone, dabbed with powder.

How can I accept it and make it work for me? Think of it as a mark that gives your face character. Many models keep a mole as a trademark (and call it a "beauty mark"). A scar shows that you were strong enough to go through something painful. Focus on the other things that are beautiful about you. When people stare, ask if they have any questions. Remember that these things are the prints left by your life as you live it.

> I look at all the other girls and say to myself, why can't I be that skinny? I wish I could be like them and wear a two-piece. I have to wear a jacket and baggy pants all summer so no one notices. I know God made us different, and he doesn't judge by appearance. I just wish other girls could be the same way he is.

Just So You Know

According to a study, twenty-six percent of ten-year-old girls are obsessed with their weight and feel they're not thin enough. Obsession ISN'T a normal part of growing up.

> Something that most people wouldn't see as an issue but I do is all my friends are white and I'm mixed race. (My dad's black, and my mom's white.) A lot of the time I feel out of place. I know that it doesn't matter what you look like and that I should wear my ethnicity with pride, but it's hard.

GOT GOD?

Even if you have the best attitude ever, there may still be kids and even adults who can't leave your glasses or your chicken pox scars or your rosy round cheeks alone. It's embarrassing. It's maddening. It's enough to make you point out *their* wart or buckteeth or bald head.

Before you hurl back an insult or run to the restroom in tears, try to remember this: When someone teases you about a "flaw," that says more about HER (or him) than it does about YOU. A mouth full of braces or a face full of freckles tells nothing about you as a person. But a rude remark from a person's mouth announces that he or she is at that moment one of these:

○ thoughtless

○ careless

○ insensitive

○ jealous

○ needing to feel better than you

○ just plain mean

So what do you do about it? God gives us four great guidelines, right in the Bible.

God's Guideline #1: Don't argue with a teaser or you'll just be teased more.

> Whoever corrects a mocker invites insults.
>
> Proverbs 9:7

God's Guideline #2: Ignore teasing. Don't even react in front of the teaser. (But it's okay to go away and cry if you need to; teasing **hurts**.)

> Fools show their annoyance at once, but the prudent overlook an insult.
>
> Proverbs 12:16

God's Guideline #3: Don't try to get back at the teaser with teasing of your own. Be your best self and compliment her honestly, help her if she needs it, and refuse to talk trash about her behind her back.

> Do not repay evil with evil or insult with insult. On the contrary, repay evil with blessing.
>
> 1 Peter 3:9

God's Guideline #4: Ask God to heal whatever is causing people to tease you until it hurts. They may not change, but YOU will. It's hard to keep hating someone you're praying for.

> "Love your enemies and pray for those who persecute you."
>
> Matthew 5:44

• •

Who, ME?

Put a big ol' cross next to the God's Guideline on the previous page that YOU are going to pray about the hardest.

YOU CAN DO IT

Talking about beauty bummers can be a downer, so let's end this chapter with an upper! "Getting the Picture" will help you see your beautiful self even MORE clearly so you can get on with this beauty journey without dragging so much baggage with you. You'll also add a new page to your travel journal that will keep you going.

What you'll need for Getting the Picture:

○ a piece of plain paper that will fit in your journal

○ colored pens, pencils, markers, crayons, whatever

○ a bold black marker or crayon

What you're doing:

You're doing what's called "getting perspective," which is what usually needs to happen when you get all upset about something. It's like stepping back and taking a fresh look so you can see that things aren't really so bad after all.

How to make it happen:

1. On your paper, draw an outline of yourself like you did in chapter 11.

2. Using COLORS, draw in all your features that you love or that you hardly even think about. *Don't use any black.* Make it as beautiful as you are.

3. Now, using BLACK, draw in anything you're not happy about.

4. Look at the final picture. There's a whole lot more color than black, isn't there? Even if you have "flaws," they have *nothing* on all that is beautiful about you. Ya gotta love that.

Now you can create a new page in your travel journal called "Banishing the Beauty Bummers." Copy the following headings onto the page and fill in the information. Be as creative as you want, of course—and feel free to decorate with comical drawings of the bummers you're banishing.

My Bummers   **Can I Change It?**
How to Make It Better   **How to Make It Work**

That's What I'm Talkin' About

Just as you've been doing at the ends of the previous chapters, journal or draw or simply think about how all the stuff you've read about applies to you. As always, you can either fill in your answers here or you can write/draw them on a page in your travel journal.

Here are this chapter's things to ponder when it's just you and God talkin':

Right now I feel different/the same/worse about my beauty bummers because _____

_____.

The next time someone teases me about it, I'm going to say _____

_____.

I never realized before that the person who teases me the most probably does it because _____

_____.

When I think about how *I* tease or comment about other people's beauty bummers, I want to say to God: _____

_____

_____.

18

What About ... ?

I just have to share this hilarious e-mail from one of your kindred mini-women. Prepare to go, "Are you *serious*?"

"I just started going to a youth group at church and, wow, the kids there have some FUNK-EEEE stuff going on.

"I saw people with lime green hair and crazy weird hair-dos and tattoos and piercings on MORE than just their ears, and their ears were covered in earrings from the tippy top down to the earlobe. It didn't look like a youth group—it looked more like some gothic gang. I just sorta stood there and stared at them."

Can't you just see it? Maybe you *have* seen it. And maybe you've even wanted to try some of that yourself, the way this tween girl did.

66 Okay, this may sound weird, but I thought I would look really pretty if I dyed my hair green. No joke. I thought people would think I was cool and want to be friends with me.

"So I got this semi-permanent lime green hair dye and put as much of it on my hair as I could. Then I rinsed it out. My hair was wet when I went to bed, so I thought nothing of the color.

"The next morning I woke up and it was seaweed green instead of lime, and it looked absolutely heinous. I was so embarrassed, but I had to go to school anyway. Everybody kept saying, 'WHAT did you do to your hair?!' So I had to keep explaining the whole thing to them all day long. I was miserable.

"And since it was semi-permanent, it lasted for a whole month and it looked awful. Thankfully I was able to exchange it for some purple hair dye, but I definitely learned to be more careful about what I try on my hair AND that I shouldn't depend so much on my outward appearance to make friends. 99

Ya think?

I could just tell you to steer away from ALL the things-that-make-parents-flip-out ...

○ tattoos

- piercings
- extreme hair styles
- clothes and accessories that scream, "Do you SEE how outrageous I am?!"

But nobody bats an eye anymore at a couple of ear piercings or a small tattoo on an ankle or a streak of maroon in the bangs, because even moms and business people are doing that. And the extreme look no longer *automatically* means that the people wearing it are "weird," "bad," or even unChristian. One mini-woman made this comment:

> My daddy has two tattoos and both of his glorify God. He has the crown of thorns on his arm and Korean letters that mean Jesus on his forearm. I kinda like that one because it spurs a lot of God conversations. People will ask him what it means, and when he tells them, I think it presents a good witnessing opportunity. But I don't think I would ever get a tattoo.

Actually, the Christian thing to do is to take a close look at the whole tattoo-piercing-etc. thing so that, for starters, you don't judge people unfairly and so you can have the best information for making your own beauty decisions when the time comes that they're yours alone to make.

Who, ME?

First thing that comes to your mind when you see somebody with a tattoo or body piercing:

_____

HERE'S THE DEAL ABOUT WHAT'S OKAY

> I don't personally think tattoos, piercings, and wild hair colors are wrong. I know people who are amazing Christians with nose rings and tats. And I don't see the difference between a green streak in a girl's hair and her mother using dye to cover up her gray.

The evidence is right in front of us that a nice Celtic cross tattoo doesn't mean the person doesn't love Jesus! What does that mean for you, the tween girl? What's okay and what's out of the question?

Okay as long as your parents give the thumbs up:

- things that aren't permanent, like fun stick-on tattoos or a feather in your hair (I've had one!)

- things you just do for fun, like wash-out hair color for a costume party

- things that REALLY show a creative side of you, like a washable marker drawing you do on your foot on a Saturday

- things that actually do show you're a Christian, like cross earrings or a tiny fish face painted on your cheek

Never okay for a tween girl (and your parents will probably agree!):

- Anything permanent, like an actual tattoo.

- Anything you do for a negative reason, like doing three ear piercings at a sleepover because your mom won't give permission to do even one.

- Anything you do just because everybody else is doing it, like wearing T-shirts with snarky sayings.

- Anything that God has said, "Don't do this."

Who, ME?

Draw a tiny picture next to any of the things in the previous OKAY and NEVER OKAY lists that YOU've thought about doing.

> My BFF wants to get a tattoo when she grows up. Personally, I think they're HEINOUS! Gross me out and make me icky!

Who, ME?

Underline any of the previous statements that have gone through YOUR mind.

> Once in a while I see some tattoos that are cute but would look better on paper or a painting or something.

HERE'S THE DEAL ABOUT THE EXTREME LOOK

Here's what I'm talking about, in more detail:

- pierced nose, tongue, lip, eyebrow, belly button

- multiple tattoos

- hair colors nobody was born with

- clothes that tell the world, "I don't care WHO you are—you aren't the boss of me."

- accessories that suggest violence or sexiness or dwell on death, like a necklace with a skull, a belt made of bullets, a top that leaves nobody guessing whatcha got under there

There are probably as many reasons for wanting to tattoo and pierce as there are people who do it. These are some of the main explanations behind decking out in all black or piercing every spot that'll hold an earring:

- "I want to be different."

- "It's my body, and I have a right to do whatever I please with it."

- "It's my way of expressing how sick I am of everybody telling me who to be."

- "I like to weird people out, especially adults who try to control me."

- "If people want to know the real me, they have to get past the way I look. If they judge me by my appearance, I don't want to know them."

- "I want people to look at me."

SO—what's wrong with that? Haven't we been saying through this whole book that you should be your unique self? That you should dress in a way that shows who you are? That you shouldn't worry about what everybody else thinks?

You're right. We have. But take a close look at each of those reasons for going for the extreme look and see why they're very different from what you've read.

"I want to be different." That's totally normal. But if all your friends or half the class are also dyeing their hair green and piercing their eyebrows, how does that make you different? It doesn't take much imagination to fit yourself into a "look."

"It's my body, and I have a right to do whatever I please with it."

That right doesn't kick in until you're at least eighteen *and* supporting yourself. Not only that, but:

- No piercing is legal without a parent being present until you're sixteen, and in some states until you're eighteen or twenty-one. Even with a parent's permission, by law a tattoo can't be done until you're eighteen. Going to someone who is willing to ignore the rules and give you a piercing or a tattoo anyway is dangerous. You can be sure that person will ignore the safety and cleanliness rules too.

- If the piercer's instruments and hands aren't totally clean, you can get an infection. That is SO not fun, especially inside your nose or mouth.

- A tattoo involves someone injecting permanent dye under your skin. If the needle isn't completely germ-free, you can get certain life-threatening diseases. It just isn't worth taking that chance.

- Even if you went to the cleanest place on the planet, there are other risks with piercing:

  ○ It's easy to swallow a tongue ring or stud.

- A belly button piercing can get infected just from getting caught on your jeans or the buttons on your shirt.

- If rings get torn out, the site can be painful. (And bloody … EW!)

- An allergic reaction can leave a permanent ring like a tattoo on your skin.

- An infection in the hard part of your ear (not the lobe) can result in your ear losing its shape and becoming deformed.

"It's my way of expressing how sick I am of everybody telling me who to be." It's actually healthy to want to be your unique self. The trick is to truly know **you** and express **that**, not your feelings. Is **bad** who you really are? Is **angry**? You might feel like nobody gets you, but there are a whole lot of healthier and safer and less permanent ways to deal with that. We'll talk about those later in this chapter.

"I like to weird people out, especially adults who try to control me." And you probably will! But what is the result? Ever noticed the way teachers watch the "bad kids"? They're always on them, ready to pounce. Teachers and other adults don't give second chances to kids who do things just to gross them out. Sometimes rebels get in trouble for things they don't even do just because they look like the type who would. Life's tough enough without inviting trouble.

"If people want to know the real me, they have to get past the way I look. If they judge me by my appearance, I don't want to know them." The whole point of looking like YOU is so people will see a real person and want to get to know you better. If you make people work that hard to see who you are inside, you waste a lot of time that could be spent sharing great friendships. Like it or not, when someone sees a girl who looks mean or tough or disrespectful, that person is going to assume she is, even if she isn't.

"I want people to look at me." We all want attention, and that isn't always a bad thing. If no one pays attention to you, you won't have friends, you won't be able to share what an awesome person you are, and you'll be pretty lonely. But you need the right **kind** of attention.

- The right kind of attention sounds like, "You're special." "I've never known anyone like you." "I like being around you because you don't try to be something you're not."

- The wrong kind of attention sounds like, "Dude, what are you trying to prove?" "I'm not inviting *her* to my party. She doesn't look like she's very nice." "I'm kinda scared of her."

It's hard if you don't get positive attention at home, and that can make you think that any kind of notice is better than none. But that isn't true. Just ahead, we'll talk about shining as the real you instead of making up somebody to be. First, let's see what might be pushing you or someone you know to go to extremes, even in the secret places in the mind.

> You can do piercings to an extent, but soon it becomes abusing your body, doesn't it?

> What happens to tattoos when you get older? Don't they go all wrinkly and fade?

> I think really extreme hairdos, like shaving your head or getting a Mohawk, doesn't mean the person is awful, but it does make them look like they hate everything.

397

> I think how we look outside reflects what's in our heart. If people are covered in tattoos, piercings, etc., they look scary. Is that what's inside them?

> The problem with people dyeing their hair bright colors or totally dark black is that they get a bad rep because they tend to add attitudes when they add color to their hair. But if you're sticking with your God-itude, I think fun colors can be super cool.

Who, ME?

What's your favorite FUN way to get the right kind of attention?

_____

_____

_____

That Is SO Me!

Put a star next to each paragraph that describes you at least *some* of the time. If the description doesn't sound like you at *all*, just leave it blank.

_____ A

I have to say, "Mom?" or "Dad!" like forever, before they answer me. It seems like my parents praise my brother (or sister) way more than they praise me. When I do things right, it's like no big deal, but if I mess something up, you would think I committed a crime. I don't think I'm good at anything. At least nobody says I am.

_____ B

Sometimes I feel like my own family doesn't get me. People say things like, "You sure aren't like your sister (or your mom or anybody else in the whole family)." Kids at school look at me like I'm weird. My parents are always trying to get me to be less this or more that (like less shy and more athletic). It doesn't really bother me that I'm kinda different, but it obviously bothers a lot of other people.

_____ C

I always have to keep my bedroom door open. If I just want to hang out by myself, people ask me what's wrong or try to make me "join in." I get in trouble for arguing, and when I want to do something new, I hear stuff like, "You're not old enough yet." There are things I want to decide for myself, but I'm not allowed to—things like how I wear my hair or what activities I do after school.

If you put a star next to any of the descriptions, you might feel …

○ **angry**

○ **frustrated**

○ **hurt**

○ **resentful**

○ **afraid**

○ **just constantly cranky**

Even if things aren't really as bad as you think they are (since most parents are doing a pretty good job), the way you see them can still make you want to punch a pillow, bite your brother, or scream at whoever happens to be standing nearby. And sometimes those thoughts and feelings can make you want to dress like a Bad Girl, wear a big ol' stud in your lip, and dye your hair some impossible color. At the very least, they can push you to hate every outfit or hairstyle your mom suggests, just because.

The thing is, lashing out at people or dressing up like a hoochie mama doesn't change those feelings. It can even make them worse because people will get so focused on the way you look, they won't discover how bad you really feel so they can help you.

Why do something that doesn't work? Let's find out what *does* work.

BTW, read the following section even if you didn't star anything on the quiz. You may have a friend who's hurting, and with this information you might be able to help her.

If you starred choice A, it sounds like you need **atten-**

tion, the kind that makes you smile and glow. The kind that nudges you to be **more** helpful, brave, friendly, or whatever it was that got people to notice you in the first place. That doesn't mean stand on a table in the cafeteria and yell, "Look at what I did!" It does mean …

- Do the things you do well because you enjoy them, not so everybody will say, "Wow."

- Discover what it is about yourself that even one person seems to like, and go with it, whether it's the way you smile, how well you listen, or the fact that you never spread gossip.

- Give other people the kind of attention *you* want: praise, sympathy, a big laugh at their jokes.

- If you're neglected by one of your parents, rather than whine or accuse, ask for some time together, even just an hour alone.

- If you don't think you do anything well, try things that sound fun or interesting to you. Have such a blast doing them that you don't worry about anyone noticing how good (or how not so good) you are at them.

- Remember that you have God's undivided attention.

If you starred choice B, maybe you're struggling to be accepted for who you really are or you're trying to **find out** who you are. That doesn't mean that whatever you do, you think everybody should say, "That's just the way she is." It means you want that calm feeling that comes when you don't have to worry whether people think you're lame or geeky or just generally strange. Try some of these:

- Don't hang out with people who make fun of you. Don't even try to be friends with them.

- Find at least one person who appreciates your special qualities or interests—your book collection, your huge vocabulary, your total love of cats. Invite her over or ask her to sit with you at lunch.

- Show your family or your classmates that the very thing they want to change in you can really be a good thing for *them*. If they say you're too quiet, listen when they have a problem. If they say you're not athletic, cheer from the sidelines when they're playing, or make a banner, or write encouraging notes if they lose. The people who love you will begin to appreciate who you are instead of trying to turn you into what they think would make you happier.

- Love who you are. Nobody is more appealing than a for-real person.

- Remember that God made your true self and is there to help you be just that.

If you starred choice C, it just may be that you want to be allowed to grow up. The adults in your life might not see that, or they think you're trying to be older too fast. It's sort of like walking around in shoes that are too small for you and pinch your toes. That doesn't mean you should ignore the limits grown-ups put on you, because you need some. But if you feel you're being treated like a baby, you can try some of these:

- Be mature in ways that are right for your age, like doing chores without having to be reminded and not slacking off in school.

- Be mature in ways that'll surprise people, like offering to watch your little brother so your mom can take a bubble bath, refusing to exclude a girl everyone else is leaving out, putting part of your allowance in the collection plate.

- Make a list of things you know aren't your decision, like what time you go to bed or whether you go to school. Then make a list of things you'd like to decide about your life, within your parents' limits, of course, maybe how you wear your hair, what books you read for fun, what sports you play. Show both lists to your parents and ask if you can make at least one of the choices on the second list.

- If you need more privacy, ask for it politely. "May I have my door closed for an hour after school?" "Could you please knock before you come in the bathroom?"

- Take care of your stuff. Keep your room at least a little bit organized. Be "together" when it's time to leave for school. Those things show that you *are* growing up.

- Dream about how you want your life to be when you're in charge of it. Some girls like to keep a journal or make a scrapbook about their imagined future.

- With your friends, or alone, pretend you're a grown-up. No matter what anybody says, you're never too old for dress-up or acting games.

- Look forward to things to come, like going to high school football games, getting a driver's license, wearing makeup, going shopping with your girl-friends, playing on a school team. But don't hurry them. Enjoy what you have right now: no money worries, time to play and daydream, permission to giggle your head off.

- Pray—a lot—for God to help you grow up at just the right rate.

- Remember that you can't rush God.

Notice that none of the suggestions above have anything to do with ...

- shocking people with your 'do.

- grossing people out with your piercings.

- making a statement with your tattoo.

- going to extremes with your clothes so people will notice you or challenge you so you can argue.

- showing zero respect for yourself because it feels like nobody *else* respects you.

Most of the suggestions we've made are positive things—do's, not don'ts. But it can be hard to do positive things when negative actions seem easier. That, of course, is why God is there for you.

Who, ME?

Who could you give some "good kind" of attention to tomorrow?

_____

Who, ME?

What were you doing the last time you said, "That's just the way I am!"

_____

_____

66 If your mom won't let you do something, it may be because she thinks you're not mature enough. Try to obey her and respect her and you might GET mature enough in her eyes. 99

Who, ME?

Write TO DO next to each of these steps that YOU need to take care of!

GOT GOD?

These are steps that will help you even if you aren't considering full tattoo sleeves or a shirt that says, "Bite Me!" After all, what mini-woman *doesn't* feel angry, frustrated, hurt, resentful, afraid, or cranky sometimes? In fact, try making this a part of your quiet time with God every day and see what happens.

Step One

Find a private place and vent to God, either out loud or in a journal or on a sketchpad, about what you're feeling, no matter what it is.

> Pour out your hearts to him, for God is our refuge.
>
> Psalm 62:8

66 I feel out of place at school sometimes. Like everyone is all into clothes and hair and vampires, and I can't join in because I'm not. I don't actually want to be doing everything that other people are but, ya know, I kinda have a little desire to be wanted and included when I'm sitting right there. Sometimes I just want to lay down on my bed and cry because I feel like I don't belong. 99

Step Two

Ask God for exactly what you need, whether it's help

sorting it all out, the courage to talk to your parents, the strength to be yourself.

> In the morning, Lord, you hear my voice;
> in the morning I lay my requests before you.
>
> Psalm 5:3

66 God? Would you please help me find a way to be included with other girls without giving up who you made me to be? IS there a way, or do I just have to be alone? 99

Step Three

Listen for God's answer. It probably isn't going to come immediately, and it may not be God's own voice. Sometimes it's a line from a song or a comment someone makes or even a movie you see. And sometimes ... you just know.

> Be strong and take heart and wait for the Lord."
>
> Psalm 27:14

66 I was struggling with not being popular because I wasn't all trendy and perfect like the girls at my school, but then I spent a weekend with my aunt. She dresses like a hippie (I think that's what you call it) and bakes bread for poor people and is always smiling. She's like the most amazing godly woman I know and I look up to her. She said when she was my age,

she didn't fit in either, and she made up her mind to only do things that honored God instead of trying to get other girls' approval. It was like a light turned on in my head. **"**

Step Four

Try your best to do what God seems to be telling you. You'll know it was really God when you see yourself becoming your more beautiful you.

> Give me understanding, so that I may keep your law and obey it with all my heart.
>
> Psalm 119:34

"So I tried that. When everybody was wearing these tiny fake tattoos with like skulls and stuff, I got one with a cross on it. And when they were all, like, 'It's summerÐtime for short-short shorts!' I just thought, no, God doesn't want me doing that. I was, like, if I have to do that to be their friend, I don't need them. It wasn't snarky, it was just, 'I'm fine.' **"**

Step Five

Repeat Steps One through Four every day. You'll get closer and closer to God and know more and more about how God wants YOU to be beautiful.

God is our refuge and strength,
an ever-present help in trouble.

Psalm 46:1

Ever since I started writing in my Talking to God Journal just about every day, I feel like God's talking to ME more. It's like I want God's voice to be louder than everybody else's.

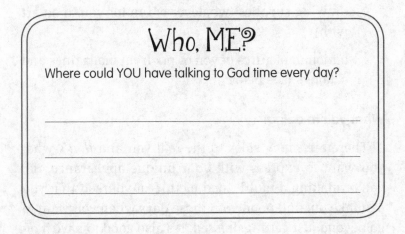

Who, ME?

Where could YOU have talking to God time every day?

_____

_____

_____

YOU CAN DO IT

The thing about using your appearance to express your feelings is that, as a mini-woman, sometimes those feelings are different every *day*—if not every *hour*! (All the more reason not to get a tattoo or sixteen piercings up your ear!) Dressing and styling your hair as who you really ARE rather than the way you FEEL is healthier (and more godly). "A Look for Every Me!" will help you with that, and so will adding a new page to your travel journal. Get ready for a way-fun leg of your beauty journey.

What you'll need for "A Look for Every Me!":

○ any kind of box that's six to twelve inches on each side (It can also be rectangular.)

○ plain paper to cover it (Colored is fun, but you can use white, brown, or black too.)

○ glue or tape

○ scratch paper

○ drawing supplies (whatever is fun for you to do art with)

○ optional: pictures of you or pix from magazines and catalogs (see below.)

What you're doing:

There are many sides to the real you and *that's* what you want to express with your unique appearance. So, you're making a multi-sided picture of yourself that you can take out and ponder on those days when you want to go beyond just getting dressed. It's also good to have it on display to remind you that there's far more to you than people (and even you!) may think.

How to make it happen:

1. Cut away the open side of the box. (Remove the lid, cut off the flaps, etc.)

2. Turn the box so that the open side is down; you should have five sides now.

3. Tape or glue the plain paper to the sides of the box.

4. On scratch paper, make a list of all the sides of YOU that you can think of.

   ○ EXAMPLES: Athlete Me, Student Me, Animal Lover Me, Dancer Me, Clown Me

5. Choose the five that you are the MOST often.

6. For each one, create a look that fits that side of you, either by drawing it (you don't have to be a great artist) or actually dressing/doing your hair/etc. that way and having someone snap a picture, or pulling it together from magazine/catalog pix. Don't forget hairstyle, accessories, maybe even fingernail polish color. You guessed it—each look goes on a different side of the box.

7. Flop yourself down in a comfy spot, and turn the box (don't forget the top) to look at the ways you can express all that you are.

Keep your box close by as you take out your travel journal and add a new page called "Looking Like Me." As always, decorate the page exactly how you want to. (Particularly important this time, right?) Then copy these headings across the top of the page and fill them in. Since this takes some thought, you might want to stretch it out over several quiet times.

My Most Comfy Look

The Looks I Like Myself Best In

"Popular" Beauty Things That Just Aren't Me

Looks I'd Like to Try To See If They're Me

That's What I'm Talkin' About

Here are this chapter's things to ponder when it's just you and God talking, writing, drawing, or adding to your travel journal.

When I'm talking to God, I want to try _____

_____

_____.

When it comes to appearance, I've changed my mind about _____

_____.

When it comes to appearance, I'm more convinced than ever that _____

_____

is true because _____

_____.

I'm still not sure about _____

_____.

One healthy, godly way to go EXTREME besides in appearance would be to _____

_____.

19

Beautiful Inside and Out

When I do beauty workshops with tween girls, I always ask; "Do you think the way you look on the outside matters at all?" The answers I get depend on whether their moms are there.

When mothers are in the room, the girls all look at each other and slowly raise their hands to say, "No. It doesn't make any difference whatsoever."

If I ask that question when there are no moms in the room, or I invite girls on the *Tween You and Me* blog to comment, I get responses like these:

"I think it matters, although not as much as inner beauty. Outward looks are, however, a part of you that God made."

"It's okay to want to be beautiful on the outside as long as it isn't your main goal. Your main goal should be being beautiful on the inside. That's what God cares about and that's the only thing that matters."

"I think it's okay to look your best as long as you don't try to dress up and put makeup on JUST so you can get attention."

"You at least want to try your best to look good, but you don't have to freak out if you don't look like other people."

"If you're a Christian but you don't take care of your body or you wear bad stuff, who's going to want to be part of YOUR religion?"

"Even God says we should look nice when we go to church and other places. We want other people to have a good impression of what a Christian is like."

"Appearance is important, like not getting overweight because then you're trashing God's wonderful creation. He loves you for who you are, though, so you shouldn't get sucked into it too much."

I wanted you to read those very TRUE statements because sometimes as Christians, we're told that what we look like on the outside doesn't matter at ALL. I think grown-ups say that because they don't want you to get obsessed with your hair and your clothes and your shape and think those are the ONLY things that count. As we said in the very first chapter of this section, that's an easy thing to start believing in this world.

Like your fellow mini-women, you probably already know that both outer beauty and inner beauty are important, and that being beautiful on the inside is the more important of the two. As in …

- It's the part God really cares about.

- It's the part that makes people truly love you.

- It's the part that can always be beautiful no matter how many bad hair days you have.

- It's the part that makes you more beautiful on the outside than makeup and hair products ever can.

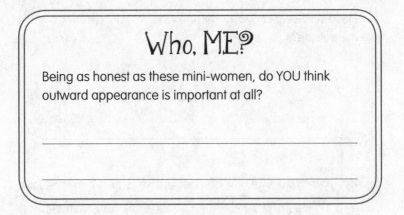

Who, ME?

Being as honest as these mini-women, do YOU think outward appearance is important at all?

_____

_____

66 When I make friends, I don't care what they look like, but appearance does matter in society, like when you go for a job interview. 99

Let's keep being honest, then. Let's face the fact that we can **say** our inside is more important and beautiful than the outside, and we can even **believe** it in our hearts. But unless we **live** it, we aren't going to be the gorgeous women we were made to be. In this final leg of our journey together, come and explore what it means to have beauty within.

> **❝**I say I don't care how people look, but I think it does change the way I act around them sometimes—like if they don't bathe or brush their hair.**❞**

Who, ME?

Have YOU ever known someone who was only pretty on the outside?

_____

_____

> **❝**I once saw a girl in Starbucks that I didn't even know, but I could see her inner beauty. She was natural and confident. Not stuck up and rude, but like she was sure of herself and laughed easily. I hope I can have that same air about myself someday.**❞**

HERE'S THE DEAL ABOUT INNER BEAUTY TRUTHS

I hope you remember everything you've read in this whole book, but if you can't, then please at least remember these very true things about beauty on the inside.

Inner Beauty Truth #1: No matter how great a girl's hair, skin, nails, and clothes are—no matter how free

she is of physical "flaws"—she will not be truly beautiful unless she shines from the inside. She might win beauty contests or get a modeling contract or have boys flocking all around her. That means she's cute, or pretty, or practically perfect from head to toe. That doesn't mean she's beautiful.

Inner Beauty Truth #2: A beautiful girl can have bad hair days, pimples, and hairy legs. She may not be able to sit still long enough to have a manicure or tweeze her eyebrows. Yet she is beautiful because she focuses on these beauty secrets:

- confidence in her God-given gifts and talents that smooth her brow

- joy that makes her eyes sparkle; honesty that makes them clear

- a sense of fun that gives her a dazzling smile

- energy in helping, sharing, and doing her best that makes her skin glow; kindness that softens it

- positive, encouraging words that make her lips lovely

- love for God, other people, and herself that makes her attractive in a way no one can explain

Who, ME?

Check off the qualities in the previous list that YOU have seen in someone.

Inner Beauty Truth #3: No matter what you look like, it is impossible to be beautiful when you are:

- sneering (curling your lip)
- taunting (hurtful teasing)
- rolling your eyes
- saying "du-uh"
- sticking out your tongue
- leering with your eyes (or giving any other mean look)
- yelling at somebody
- gossiping
- smiling without meaning it

Try doing any of the above in a mirror and you'll see what I mean.

Inner Beauty Truth #4: You can't be beautiful if you hate yourself. When you hate someone else, your mouth gets hard and your eyes squint down and the skin pinches in between your eyebrows, and no amount of skin care and cute clothes can make that pretty. Why would it be any different if you despise yourself? If you really, really can't stand who you are, please talk about that with a grown-up you trust. You MUST find out that you are every bit as lovable as every one of God's other creations. I mean it.

Inner Beauty Truth #5: If you make it a point to see the beauty inside of other people, you'll be beautiful too. Like so many of God's mysteries, that's one that can't be explained.

Let's try some experiments that will show you that all those truths are, well, true!

> Sometimes (not all the time) girls who are involved in sports and are just competing again and again and again develop this harshness about them. It doesn't look good on them.

> I feel so ugly sometimes, but then that's when God comes close to me and whispers in my ear that I'm beautiful.

Who, ME?

On a scale of 1 to 5 (5 being the most) how much do YOU like you?

_____

> It's too bad other people don't know what inner beauty is ...

> Sometimes girls everybody thinks are pretty look like they're angry at the world and that makes them not pretty anymore.

That Is SO Me!

Experiment #1:

Pick out a few girls you know who are considered cute
or pretty. Watch them whenever you can. If you see one
being rude to someone or using bad language, watch even
more closely. Is she still pretty? What if someone caught
her on camera at that moment? Would a magazine put it
on the cover?

Experiment #2:

Go through a magazine you can tear pages out of. Col-
lect all the pictures of what you think are pretty women
or girls. Then put them in two piles: (1) girls you'd like
to be friends with, and (2) girls you might steer clear of.
What's the difference? Which pile shows truly beautiful
girls (from what you can tell)?

Experiment #3:

Make a list of the people you love. Next to each one,
write in a few words why you love that person so much.
Then picture each one in your mind or look at the person
for real if you can. Do you see any of those people as ugly?

Experiment #4:

Tell a person you love why you feel that way about her. Watch her face and see if it doesn't become even more beautiful than it already was.

Wouldn't it be great if you could just say, "From now on, I am going to be confident, joyful, fun-loving, energized, kind, encouraging, and loving"? It would be like an instant beauty treatment!

Yeah, well, developing those qualities takes time, and it takes God. We can't do it by reading books or following rules or copying women we admire, although those things help. So what DO we do?

❝All I want to do is radiate inner beauty to everyone.❞

❝If people act like Jesus would, the outside doesn't matter.❞

GOT GOD?

If you do these things every day just the way you do the things on your Beauty Chart, God will give you a beauty treatment that will last a lifetime.

> "'Love the Lord your God with all your heart and with all your soul and with all your mind.' This is the first and greatest commandment. And the second is like it: 'Love your neighbor as yourself.'"
>
> Matthew 22:37–39

- Worship and pray and hang out with God.

- Love other people the way you want to be loved.

- Know your real self and take care of her.

> Whatever is true, whatever is noble, whatever is right, whatever is pure, whatever is lovely, whatever is admirable—if anything is excellent or praiseworthy—think about such things … put it into practice.
>
> Philippians 4:8–9

- Watch inspiring movies, listen to great music, go to beautiful natural places, read wonderful books—the things that make you want to be your best self.

- Get to know people you look up to.

- Go for things that really matter.

> Be like-minded, be sympathetic, love one another, be compassionate and humble. Do not repay evil with evil or insult with insult. On the contrary, repay evil with blessing.
>
> 1 Peter 3:8–9

- Do your best to get along with people without giving up who you are.

- Try to understand why people are hard to be with sometimes.

- Be there when someone needs you.

- Don't think you're better than anybody else.

- Ignore the bullies when they taunt you—and then pray for them.

Can't you just feel yourself becoming more beautiful already?

● ●

Who, ME?

How many inches more beautiful do you feel now than when you started reading this chapter?

_____

66 I think I'm beautiful on the inside because I always give people second chances. 99

66 I love the way I can just totally sympathize with people and cry with them and comfort them and hug them without caring what other people around us think. 99

66 My shyness and quietness are beautiful. 99

66 My inner beauty comes from my bubbly confidence and creativity. 99

YOU CAN DO IT

Living out your inner beauty takes attention and practice. This "Inner Beauty Treatment" will help you get started, and creating the next (but not final!) page in your travel journal will keep you going. Forever.

What you'll need for Inner Beauty Treatment:

1. A quiet, private place where you can get really comfortable.

2. At least thirty minutes (This works best at night before bed if you can manage that.).

3. Your all-time favorite snack on a pamper-yourself plate.

4. This book or your travel journal in case you can't write answers here.

5. Paper to write two notes (You get to choose what kind.).

6. Bathtub, water, and bubble bath—OR shower, body wash, and loofah or washcloth—OR a sink and some warm water and face wash.

7. Your bed!

What you're doing:

You're learning how to love yourself in a healthy, unselfish way.

How to make it happen:

Just follow the suggestions in each Treatment step. You might want to read through all of them first so you can flow right through.

Step One: Be compassionate to yourself.

- "I am going to stop beating myself up about _____."

- Give yourself a huge hug. (Go ahead—no one's watching!)

Step Two: Be honest with yourself.

- "I am mean to myself when I _____ _____."

- Write yourself a letter of apology, with a promise to stop.

Step Three: Stand up for yourself.

- "I am going to stop allowing _____ _____."

- Make a promise to yourself. Out loud. Even if you have to whisper.

Step Four: Be humble about yourself.

- "I give God all the credit for my _____ _____."

- Write God a thank-you note, and put it in your Bible or your travel journal.

○ **Step Five: Repay yourself for a mistake with a blessing.**

- "I forgive myself for _____ _____."

- Take a luxurious cleansing bath or an invigorating shower or do a lovely face washing.

○ **Step Six: Be sympathetic with yourself.**

- "I feel bad for myself because _____ _____."

- Climb into bed, and let God rock you to sleep.

Tomorrow, make a new page in your travel journal called "I'm on My Way." As always, decorate it however you want to. Then describe the person you know you are deep inside, with all her God-made inner qualities. Ah—isn't she lovely?

That's What I'm Talkin' About

One of your fellow mini-women wrote this poem that she's given me permission to share with you.

I am God's own child, perfect in his sight,

Set apart for a purpose: to shine and spread his light.

Yet I try to fit in with the popular teens.

I buy the latest fashion, forgetting what true beauty means.

But lovingly and quietly, God whispers in my ears

That I was not created to "fit in" with my peers.

He told me I'm a princess, because he is the king;

I am his daughter and he's my everything.

What an honor it is to have a Father King

So I've nothing to be ashamed of. To this truth I cling:

I'm ambassador from heaven, here to spread God's light,

Have this glow inside me; hiding it wouldn't be right.

I'll be a friend to friendless, shine light into dark parts,

Do it all in Jesus' name, let God work in their hearts.

Now close this book, breathe God in, and listen. In the silence God will tell you what I told you when we started this journey together.

You. Are. Beautiful.

God bless you, mini-woman.

Talk It Up!

Want free books?
First looks at the best new fiction?
Awesome exclusive merchandise?

We want to hear from you!

Give us your opinions on titles, covers, and stories.
Join the Z Street Team.

Email us at zstreetteam@zondervan.com
to sign up today!

Also—Friend us on Facebook!

www.facebook.com/goodteenreads

- Video Trailers

- Connect with your favorite authors

- Sneak peeks at new releases

- Giveaways

- Fun discussions

- And much more!